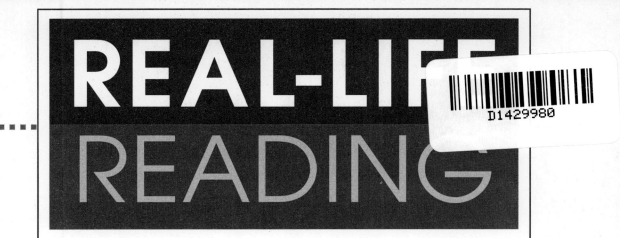

REAL-LIFE READING

by
Tara McCarthy

SCHOLASTIC
PROFESSIONAL**B**OOKS

**New York • Toronto • London • Auckland • Sydney
Mexico City • New Delhi • Hong Kong • Buenos Aires**

Photography: PhotoDisk/Getty Images
Illustrations: Mona Mark
Cover design by Solás
Interior design by Solás

ISBN: 0- 439-23776-9
Copyright © 2002 by Scholastic, Inc.
All rights reserved
Printed in the U.S.A.
3 4 5 6 7 8 9 10   40   09 08 07 06 05 04

REAL-LIFE READING

CONTENTS

To the Teacher

Real Life Reading is designed to help young adults develop and apply basic reading skills to their everyday encounters with the written word. These encounters cover a wide range: from reading road signs, bus schedules, and classified ads, to reading and understanding instructions for taking a test, using a checking account, and filling out a job application. The lessons will be of particular value to ESL students, as well as to native English speakers who need intensive practice in close-reading skills. Here are the main features of the program:

1. The lesson format is supportive. Students first work with you and fellow classmates to preview, discuss, and practice the skill.

2. Key words from each lesson are listed and defined under Words and Meanings. For example, the lesson on reading classified advertisements lists and defines common abbreviations found in these ads.

3. Students immediately practice the skill on their own. The second page of each lesson, Use What You've Learned, encourages independent practice and application of the skill or concept.

4. In each section, a midway review and a final test allow you and the student to check comprehension and identify any concepts or skills that need to be revisited.

Suggested Procedure

1. Teacher works with the class
   - to read and discuss the first page of each lesson and to answer questions.
   - to clarify what students must do independently on the second page.

2. Students work independently
   - to complete Use What You've Learned.
   - to check their responses with a partner.

3. Teacher works with the class

   ■ to identify correct answers to Use What You've Learned and to discuss why they are correct.
   ■ to discuss any uncertainties or questions students encounter as they apply the particular skill.

Ways of Sharing

1. Encourage students to bring in real-life examples to discuss with the class. For example, a student might bring in a bus schedule, a sale announcement, or a job application. Show the example on an overhead projector and invite students to discuss it according to the criteria presented in the lesson.

2. Encourage students to relate anecdotes—real or imagined—about what happened as a result of someone misreading or ignoring a sign or an instruction. Welcome humor along with the nitty-gritty. Examples: By misreading a road sign, a traveler might end up spending the night lost in a swamp instead of at a motel; by not filling out an order form correctly, a customer might end up with 100 T-shirts instead of one T-shirt.

In conclusion, take advantage of any opportunity to write instructions on the chalkboard rather than communicating them aloud. Then invite students to read these instructions aloud, discuss them, and carry them out.

section 1

Reading and traveling go together!

If you want to travel safely, you have to read and obey road signs and symbols.

If you want to get to places on time, you have to read and understand schedules.

If you're walking or driving, you have to read street and road maps to find the most direct route from here to there.

In this section, you can put your reading skills to work to become a skillful traveler, too.

Contents

1. The Shapes of Road Signs

Good drivers look ahead for the **shapes** of signs. Then they're prepared for the messages in the signs.

A road sign in one of these shapes gives a WARNING.

A sign in this shape shows a DESTINATION or direction.

EXIT 43

SERVICE AREA

A sign in this shape gives a REGULATION or traffic law.

TOLL AHEAD

EXIT SPEED 25

MAXIMUM SPEED 60

Words and Meanings

detour—a road used instead of the main road

exit—a way to leave the road you're on

maximum speed—highest legal speed

resume speed—you can go back to the legal speed limit

service area—rest area, gas station, food

toll—money required to drive on some roads

yield—let the car coming toward you go first. If you are entering a traffic circle, the car on the circle should go first.

1. Which sign would have the words **TO WASHINGTON, D.C.?**

   a   b   c

2. Which sign will have a **warning** message in it?

   a   b   c

3. Which sign will indicate a **traffic law**?

   a   b   c

4. Which sign warns about trains that may cross the road?

   a   b   c

5. The sign says **DETOUR—2 mi AHEAD**. That means:

   a   the road ahead is only two miles long.

   b   in two miles, you will be in Detour City.

   c   in two miles, you will turn onto another road.

6. You don't want to go the wrong way on a one-way road. Which sign do you watch for?

   a   b   c

7. You need food. The car needs gas. Which sign do you watch for?

   a   b   c

8. Study the picture at right. Answer these two questions.

   Which car must wait?

   _____

   _____

   How do you know?

   _____

   _____

   _____

2. Symbols on Road Signs

A symbol is a **picture** that gives a **message**. Study the symbols on the road signs below.

 An **arrow** shows which **way to go**.

 There is a **railroad crossing**.

 Traffic must **yield**.

 Traffic must **stop**.

 No **U–turn** allowed.

 No **left turn** allowed.

 School children are **crossing** here.

 There is an intersection.

One very important symbol is painted on the road itself. It's the line down the middle.

A solid line, or two solid lines, means: ━━━━━━━━

Do NOT pass the car in front of you.

A broken line means: ▬ ▬ ▬ ▬ ▬ ▬ ▬ ▬ ▬

You may pass the car ahead of you IF another car is not coming toward you.

1. This arrow tells you to

   a turn right.
   b turn left.
   c go straight ahead.

2. This arrow tells you

   a you can turn here to go in the opposite direction.
   b you cannot turn left here.
   c the road ahead is closed.

3. Which sign means
   SCHOOL CHILDREN CROSS THE ROAD HERE?

   a  b   c

4. In the picture below, a policeman has pulled
   this car over to the side. The policeman says
   to the driver, "Didn't you notice the solid line?"
   Evidently the driver

   a passed a car in a no-passing part of the road.
   b was going over the speed limit.
   c did not slow down in a school crossing area.

Look at the picture below. Look carefully at the shapes of the five different signs. Each shape has a number. Read the questions. Circle the correct answers.

5. Which symbol is inside sign 5?

   a   b   c

6. Which words are in sign 4?
   a do not enter
   b one way
   c no u-turn

7. Which symbol will most likely be found inside
   sign 2?

   a   b   c

8. Signs 1 and 3 probably show
   a advertisements.
   b directions to another town.
   c traffic regulations.

3. Busy Streets

There are many **traffic signs** on busy streets. If you don't **obey** the signs, here are some things that might **happen**:

- You could cause an accident and injure someone.

- The police could give you a traffic ticket and you would have to pay a fine.

- Your car could get towed away by the police, and you would have to pay a fine in order to get your car back.

Words and Meanings

dead end—the road ends just ahead. There's no exit at the other end.

emergency—a dangerous situation

fine—money you pay if you break a law

intersection—the point where two roads cross

loading/unloading zone—place where trucks park. If you're not driving a truck, don't park here!

no standing—no waiting and no parking allowed here. Just pick up what you have to pick up and move along.

route—a road

tow—haul or pull

traffic violation—breaking a traffic law

zone—a section, place, or area. For example, SCHOOL ZONE means a place where school children are likely to be crossing the street.

1. You park your car next to this sign. You get a ticket because:

   a cars are allowed to park here only at certain times.

   b cars are not allowed to park here at all.

   c the driver is driving a bus.

2. The police stop a car that has crossed an **intersection**—a place where two roads meet. The driver gets a ticket. Which sign might the driver have missed?

a   **b**   **c**

3. It is 10:00 a.m. on Saturday. By which sign can you safely park your car?

a NO PARKING EXCEPT SUNDAY **b** NO PARKING 8AM-6PM MON WED FRI **c** NO PARKING LOADING AND UNLOADING ONLY

4. A car is being pulled away by a police tow truck. Where did the driver park the car?

   a at a SCHOOL zone

   b at a TOW AWAY zone

   c at a BUSY INTERSECTION zone

5. Who gets a ticket?

   a   b

Explain your choice.

_____

_____

6. Which car gets a ticket?

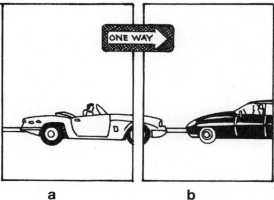

   a   b

Explain your choice.

_____

_____

13

4. Getting a Driver's License

It's not easy to get a **driver's license**. Here are the **main rules** in most states:

1. You must be at least 16 years old.

2. You must pass certain tests:

   - **A vision test:** How well can you see? Do you need glasses in order to drive safely?

   - **A written test:** You will get a driver's book to study. You have to learn the safety rules in it before taking the test. If you pass this test, you get a **learner's permit**.

3. Now, as a **learner**, you can **practice** driving, but only if you have a driver with you who already has a license.

4. When you think you're ready, you take a **road test**. A person from the State Department of Motor Vehicles will ride with you to see how well you drive. The inspector will watch to see if you do the following:

   - Signal before you make a turn.

   - Obey speed limit signs, traffic lights, and stop signs.

   - Look to the left or right before changing lanes.

   - Park your car correctly and quickly.

5. Now you're ready to fill in your driver's license application. It will be similar to the one on the next page.

DRIVER'S LICENSE APPLICATION
Use blue or black ink only in the boxes.

FOR OFFICE USE ONLY
Batch file No.
T-code
LRC   LAM   LRN
LOP

Do not write anything here.

A. LAST NAME   FIRST NAME   MIDDLE INITIAL

Do not use a pencil or red ink or green ink.

B. DATE OF BIRTH   **SEX**   **HEIGHT**   **EYE COLOR**   **SOCIAL SECURITY NUMBER**
Month   Day   Year   M   F   Ft. Inches

C. MAILING ADDRESS *(Include Street Number and Name, Rural Delivery, Box and/or Apartment Number)*

CITY OR TOWN   STATE   ZIP CODE   COUNTY

A post office box won't do. Write your home address.

D. Do you have or have you held a driver's license for this state?   ☐ No   ☐ Yes

If YES, write the license number.

E. Sign your name in full

To answer YES, put a check mark in the box before YES. To answer NO, put a check mark in the box before NO.

Please help Mary Lee Yen fill in the driver's license application above.

1. Fill in line A for Mary Lee Yen, according to the directions.

2. Use these facts to fill in line B:
    Mary Lee Yen was born on January 2, 1983. She's a female, and she's five feet four inches tall. She has green eyes. Her Social Security number is 958-24-9687.

3. Use these facts to fill in C:
    Mary Lee Yen gets her mail at 5 Dulcimer Lane, Apartment A, in Woodstock, New York. The zip code there is 12498. That's in Ulster County.

4. Mary has never had a driver's license. Fill in D to show this.

5. On line E, sign the name that should appear there.

5. Reading a Street Map

Whether you're **driving** or **walking** through a city that's new to you, a **street map** helps you find your way. The first thing to know is that a good map has a **compass rose**, like this.

Find the compass rose on the street map of Washington, D.C., below. Notice how the compass rose helps you figure out directions. For example, you can see that Massachusetts Avenue is to the **north** of Constitution Avenue; and that Delaware Avenue is to the **east** of 3rd Street.

In which direction would you travel to get from Constitution Avenue to Independence Avenue?

Does New Jersey Avenue run from east to west, or from north to south?

■ A map may also have a KEY. Find the key on the map below. The key tells you exactly where important things are located. For example, the circled number ③ before *Library of Congress* tells you to look for ③ on the map to find the location of the Library.

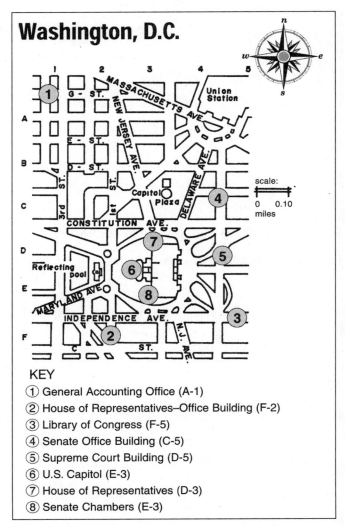

Washington, D.C.

scale:
0   0.10
miles

KEY
① General Accounting Office (A-1)
② House of Representatives–Office Building (F-2)
③ Library of Congress (F-5)
④ Senate Office Building (C-5)
⑤ Supreme Court Building (D-5)
⑥ U.S. Capitol (E-3)
⑦ House of Representatives (D-3)
⑧ Senate Chambers (E-3)

Words and Meanings

map title—it tells you what the map is about

compass rose—it shows directions: north, south, east, west

map scale—it's used to measure distances on the map

map key—it gives you the meaning of numbers used on the map

In the next lesson, you will learn about the map scale and more about the map key. You will also learn how to use the numbers at the top of the map and the letters down the side.

1. Constitution Avenue runs from
   a east to west.
   b north to south.

2. G Street is _____ of D Street.
   a south
   b north

3. Which of these is the best way to describe Massachusetts Avenue?
   a It slants from north to southeast.
   b It goes directly from north to south.

4. If you walk south on Delaware Avenue, you'll come to
   a Constitution Avenue.
   b New Jersey Avenue.

5. According to the key, ⑤ shows the location of
   a the House of Representatives.
   b the Supreme Court Building.
   c Delaware Avenue.

6. The *Office* Building of the House of Representatives is at
   a ⑤
   b ⑦
   c ②

7. To get from the Senate Office Building to the Supreme Court Building you will walk
   a east.
   b north.
   c south.

8. The government building that is farthest to the **north** on this map is
   a the Senate Chambers.
   b the U.S. Capitol.
   c the General Accounting Office.

9. Look at the map. Imagine you are coming out of the U.S. Capitol facing west with two friends. Next, you want to visit the House of Representatives. Friend A says, "We have to go straight ahead." Friend B says, "No, we have to turn left." You say, "No we have to turn right." Who is correct?
   a you
   b friend A
   c friend B

10. Look at the map on page 16. Imagine you are walking **east** on Constitution Avenue. At the corner of 1st Street, a tourist who's also walking east asks you, "How do I get to the House of Representatives?" Using the map, write the directions you would give to the tourist. Be as brief and accurate as you can.

_____

_____

_____

_____

In this lesson, you will continue learning about maps, this time **focusing** on **distances** and **locations**.

■ Look at the **Scale.** It's designed to show **distances**, or how far it is from one place to another. Some travelers would use a ruler, but you can use your finger with this scale to figure distances. This scale goes from 0 to $\frac{1}{10}$ of a mile.

■ Look at the **Key.** The **letter** and **number** *after* each place name show *another* way of finding a **location** on the map. You'll see the numbers across the top of the map and the letters down the lefthand side. Read across and down. The place where the letter and number meet shows a location. For example, the location of the House of Representatives is D-3. You can also use the numbers and letters to tell about locations *not* listed in the Key. For example, Union Station is at A-4.

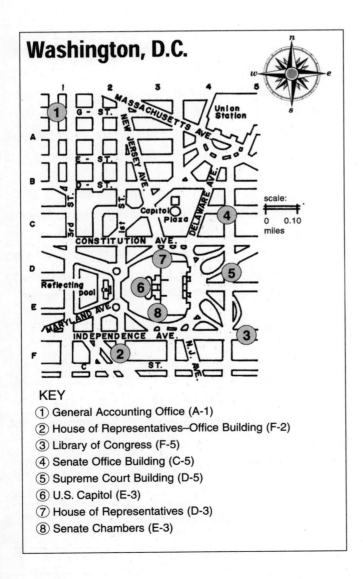

Washington, D.C.

scale:
0   0.10
miles

KEY
① General Accounting Office (A-1)
② House of Representatives–Office Building (F-2)
③ Library of Congress (F-5)
④ Senate Office Building (C-5)
⑤ Supreme Court Building (D-5)
⑥ U.S. Capitol (E-3)
⑦ House of Representatives (D-3)
⑧ Senate Chambers (E-3)

1. About how far is the General Accounting Office from the Senate Office Building?
   a about 4/10 of a mile
   b about 10 miles
   c about 1/10 of a mile

2. About how far is it from the U.S. Capitol to the House of Representatives?
   a about 1/10 of a mile
   b about 1 mile
   c about 7 miles

3. Find the **Reflecting Pool** on the map. Now read across and down. The pool is at
   a C-1.   b F-1.   c D-1.

4. What important area will you find at C-3?
   a Constitution Avenue
   b Capitol Plaza
   c Union Station

5. Where does New Jersey Avenue meet Independence Avenue?
   a at F-4   b at C-3   c at A-2

6. Where does 1st Street meet Maryland Avenue?
   a E-1   b C-2   c E-2

7. Which streets run from **east** to **west**?
   a all the streets that have state names
   b all the streets that have letter names, like G
   c all the streets that have number names, like 1st

Follow the directions.

8. F Street is not labeled on the map, but you can figure out where it is. On the map, write **F Street** where it belongs.

9. 2nd Street is not labeled on the map. On the map write **2nd Street** where it belongs.

10. Imagine that you've just arrived at Union Station in Washington, D.C. You have *three* hours to spend in Washington before you must board your next train, so you're going to *walk* around and see just two or three of the sights shown on the map. Within the time that you have, which places can you visit without rushing too much? Use the map scale and the numbers and letters to help you plan your walk. Then write your sight seeing plan below.

    Don't forget to figure in the time it will take you to walk back to Union Station!

    _____

    _____

    _____

    _____

    _____

    _____

    _____

    _____

A **highway** is a main public road that connects towns and cities.

An **interstate highway** is a highway that connects **states**.

An interstate highway number is shown in a symbol like this:

INTERSTATE

■ Find **15** on the map below. Note that if you started at
Interstate 15 in the state of **Montana**, and followed it all the
way **south**, you'd end up at the southernmost point in the state of **California**.

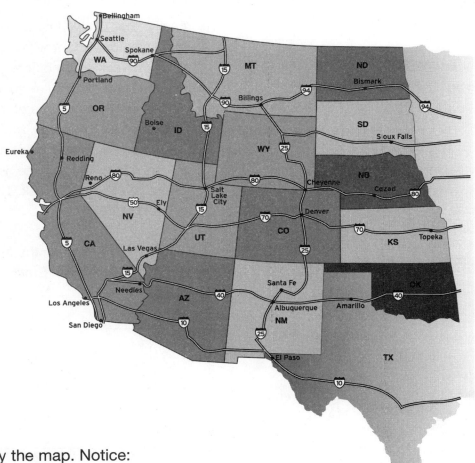

Study the map. Notice:

- ■ An interstate highway number that *ends* in an *odd* number, such as 1, 3, 5, 7, or 9, like **25**, indicates a highway that goes from **north** to **south**.

- ■ An interstate highway number that *ends* in an *even* number, such as 0, 2, 4, 6, or 8, like **24**, indicates a highway that goes from **east** to **west**.

1. **5** goes **north** from Los Angeles, California, to

   a San Diego, California.
   b Eureka, California.
   c Bellingham, Washington.

2. The best route **to** Seattle, Washington, **from** Cheyenne, Wyoming, is

   a Interstate 80 West.
   b Interstate 25 North to Interstate 90 West.
   c Interstate 80 West to Interstate 15 North.

3. If you drive east on **40** from Needles, California to Albuquerque, New Mexico, you will also go through the state of

   a Nevada.   b Utah.   c Arizona.

4. You can take **80** all the way from Cozad, Nebraska to

   a Ely, Nevada.
   b Reno, Nevada.
   c Eureka, California.

5. You're driving west on from Bismarck, North Dakota. Your destination is Spokane, Washington. At Billings, Montana, you note that **94** changes to

   a   b   c

6. Which interstate highway is farthest north?

   a   b **90**   c

7. Which interstate highway is farthest east?

   a **5**   b **25**   c **15**

8. Imagine that you're planning to drive from Amarillo, Texas, to Redding, California. Tell the routes you will take, including details like north, south, east, and west. Name some of the cities you will pass through on your trip west.

   _____

   _____

   _____

   _____

8. Symbols Across the Country

As you learned on pages 8 and 9, symbols are pictures that provide you with information. The **symbols** in signs along roads and highways are **useful** because:

- They have an agreed-upon meaning that is the same from state to state.

- Drivers can read a symbol quickly.

- The meanings of the symbols are clear, no matter what language the driver speaks.

Below is a list of commonly used symbols on signs around the country.

 Campground

 Foot Trail

 Forest Ranger Station

 Airport

 Deer Crossing

 Information

 Traffic in Both Directions Ahead

 Picnic Area

 Gas Station Ahead

 Maximum Vehicle Height

Words and Meanings

campground—a place where you can pitch a tent and stay overnight

forest ranger—an officer in charge of protecting a public forest

foot trail—a trail for hikers

scenic route—a road from which you can see beautiful sights

1. Which symbol means "Drivers can get information here"?

   a   b   c

2. Which symbol means "This way to the airport"?

   a   b   c

3. Which symbol means "Picnic Area"?

   a   b   c

4. Which symbol means "Railroad Crossing"?

   a   b   c

5. Study the symbols below. Draw a line from each symbol to its correct meaning.

   a   Picnic Area

   b   Gas Station

   c   Intersection

6. Complete the paragraph with the words or phrases that are correct.

   We stopped here

   to get _____ .

         directions
         something to eat

   We wanted to find

   _____ .

         the airport
         a place to camp

Vocabulary

Choose the best meaning for the word or words in dark letters. Circle your answers.

1. A **detour** is
   a a place to get gas for your car.
   b a road to use instead of the main road.
   c a place to see beautiful sights.

2. A **school zone** is a place where
   a school children cross the road.
   b drivers are not allowed.
   c your car can get towed away.

3. An **intersection** is
   a a road that has no exit at the other end.
   b a place where two or more roads meet.
   c a place where trucks park to load or unload.

4. **Yield** means
   a to pay a toll.
   b to resume the legal speed limit.
   c to let the other car on the road go first.

5. In most states, to get a **driver's license**, you must
   a prove that you own a car.
   b take only a written test.
   c be at least 16 years old.

6. The **vision test** for a driver's license checks how well you can
   a hear.   b drive.   c see.

7. During the **road test**, the examiner will pay the most attention to
   a whether you obey signs, speed limits, and traffic lights.
   b whether the car is clean and in good condition.
   c how well you answer questions about your driving experiences.

8. Which of the following is a **compass rose**?

   a   b   c

9. A **map scale** helps you figure out
   a the *distance* from one place to another.
   b the *direction* to travel from one place to another.
   c where different *roads meet* on a road map.

10. An **interstate highway** is a highway that
    a goes from one state to another.
    b begins and ends in the same state.
    c only goes from north to south.

11. A **map key**
    a tells you the meaning of numbers and letters on a map.
    b shows you the main roads from one place to another.
    c shows you directions, such as north, south, east, and west.

12. A **symbol** is a
    a name for a road or highway.
    b line on a map.
    c picture that stands for something.

Comprehension

Study each picture. Circle the correct answer for the a's. Write the answer for b's.

1.

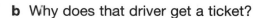

a Which driver gets a ticket?

the black car   the white car

b Why does that driver get a ticket?

_____

_____

_____

2. **a** You turned off from the road you were on because you saw which sign?

b What would *you* do to find a road that would help you continue on your journey?

_____

_____

_____

3.

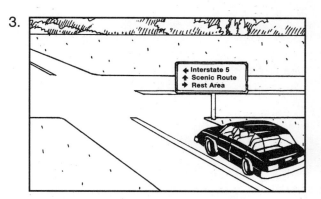

Which way should the driver go to get to a **Rest Area**?

left   right   straight ahead

4. What is the most important thing *you've* learned about highway symbols?

_____

_____

_____

_____

_____

_____

_____

_____

9. Reading a Bus Schedule

A **schedule** tells about **time**. A **bus schedule** tells the time when buses **depart** (leave) a place and **arrive** at (get to) another place.

Many bus schedules also tell the **frequency** (how often) a particular bus operates. For example, some buses may only operate from Monday to Friday, while others buses may only operate on Saturdays and Sundays.

Practice reading a bus schedule using the schedule below.

ADIRONDACK TRAILWAYS

DEPARTURES FROM KINGSTON, N.Y., TO NEW YORK, N.Y.			RETURN FROM NEW YORK, N.Y., TO KINGSTON, N.Y.		
DEPART	ARRIVE	FREQUENCY	DEPART	ARRIVE	FREQUENCY
545A	805A	X67	700A	905A	Daily
600A	820A	1	830A	1035A	Daily
645A	845A	Daily	1000A	1205P	Daily
720A	935A	Daily	1230P	235P	Daily
830A	1035A	Daily	135P	335P	X7
930A	1135A	X7	200P	405P	Daily
1030A	1235P	Daily	330P	535P	Daily
1230P	235P	Daily	500P	705P	Daily
245P	440P	7	600P	805P	Daily
300P	505P	Daily	600P	805P	5
530P	735P	7	700P	905P	5
530P	735P	Daily	730P	935P	7
730P	935P	7	800P	1005P	Daily
730P	935P	Daily	930P	1135P	Daily
1000P	1205A	7	1130P	135A	Daily
1130P	135A	Daily			

SCHEDULES SUBJECT TO CHANGE WITHOUT NOTICE.
FOR MORE INFORMATION CALL 1-800-555-8555

1—MON	3—WED	5—FRI	7—SUN	X—EXCEPT
2—TUES	4—THURS	6—SAT	H—HOLIDAY	

Words and Meanings

A—a.m., or morning (12:01 to 12 noon)

P—p.m., or afternoon and evening (12:01 to 12 midnight)

arrive—get to

depart—leave

frequency—when; how often

return—go back

Read down the first column.

What does this column tell you?

Read down the second column.

What does this column tell you?

Read down the third column.

What does this column tell you?

1. A bus leaves Kingston at 6:45 a.m. At what time does it arrive in New York City?

   a At 7:20 a.m.

   b At 8:45 a.m.

   c At 6:00 p.m.

2. What does *Daily* means on the bus schedule?

   a every day of the week

   b only in the morning

   c only on weekends

3. Look at the clues at the bottom of the schedule. You can get a 6:00 a.m. bus from Kingston to New York City

   a only on Monday.

   b any day of the week.

   c only on a holiday.

4. Look at the clues at the bottom of the schedule. **X67** means:

   a extra bus on Saturdays and Sundays.

   b except on Saturdays and Sundays.

   c bus operates only on holidays.

5. The 2:45 p.m. bus from Kingston to New York City operates:

   a 7 days a week.

   b only on Sunday.

   c every afternoon.

6. Imagine that you live in New York City. You have a job interview in Kingston, New York, at 12 noon. To be **sure** to be on time for your interview, which bus will you take from New York City?

   a the 730P   b the 830A   c the 1000A

7. A friend in New York City has asked you to come to his Saturday night party. You say that you will attend, but you have to be back home in Kingston by midnight. Which bus will you have to catch to get home just in time?

   a the 1000A   b the 1130P   c the 930P

8. Imagine that you're organizing a museum trip to New York City from Kingston. The group will travel by bus. Your group must be at the New York City Museum at 10:00 in the morning. The group must be back home in Kingston by 11:00 that night. The bus trip takes about two hours. Use the bus schedule on page 26 to fill in the blanks below with the correct times.

   We will meet in Kingston to take the bus that leaves at_____.
   720A   930A   1000P
   We will arrive in New York City at:

   _____.
   905A   935A   1035P

   Enjoy the museum! But remember that we all have to be back in Kingston by 11:00 p.m. After supper, please meet at the bus station so we can catch the bus that leaves for Kingston at _____.
   1000A   330P   800P

10. Reading a Train Schedule

A train schedule, or timetable, shows the times when trains leave and arrive at certain places. A train schedule also provides travelers with other important information about the train. The schedule below tells about trains that start in New York City and make a final stop in Washington, D.C. Study the schedule and the notes about it.

TRAIN NAME		Metroliner Service	Charter Oak	Metroliner Service
TRAIN NUMBER		125	647	127
DAYS OF OPERATION		Daily Ex Sa	Daily	Daily Ex Fr Su
TRAIN SERVICE		R ☎ ☕ ●	☕	R ☎ ☕ ●
New York, NY	Dp	6 00P	6 30P	7 00P
Newark, NJ		R 6 13P	6 44P	R 7 13P
Baltimore, MD		8 14P	9 05P	9 19P
New Carrollton, MD	↓	D 8 41P	9 33P	D 9 46P
Washington, DC	Ar	8 55P	9 50P	9 55P

Legend:
  R Stops only to receive passengers
  D Stops only to discharge passengers
  R All reserved train
  ☎ Railfone public telephone service
  ● Club Service
  ☕ Sandwiches, snack and beverage service

— train name
— train number
— days when the train runs
— See the *Legend* for meanings of the symbols here.
Dp means *depart,* or leave.
This arrow points down. It means "Read down on the schedule."
Ar means *arrive.*

These are symbols used in this timetable. After each symbol, you see its meaning. For example R stands for **All reserved train**. That means you have to go to a *reservation* counter at the train station and get your ticket *before* you get on the train.

Words and Meanings

club service—you can buy a full meal on the train

discharge—passengers get off the train

Ex Fr Su—except Fridays and Sundays

Ex Sa—except Saturday

receive—passengers get on the train

Use the train schedule on this page to answer the questions below.

1. To know the times for stops from New York to Washington, you read
   a across the timetable.
   b down the timetable.
   c up the timetable.

2. If you take the Metroliner Service at six in the evening (6 00 P, or p.m.) from New York, what time will you arrive in Baltimore?
   a 8:55 p.m.   b 7:00 p.m.   c 8:14 p.m.

3. What train will you take to go to Trenton, N.J.?
   a Metroliner Service 125
   b Charter Oak 647
   c Metroliner Service 127

4. To get to Philadelphia by 7:30 p.m. from New York, which train will you take?
   a Metroliner Service 125.
   b Metroliner Service 127.
   c Charter Oak 647.

5. Which train has *only* sandwiches and snacks?
   a Metroliner Service 125
   b Charter Oak
   c Metroliner Service 127

6. On train 125, how long is the ride from New York to Washington?
   a 3 hours 20 minutes
   b 2 hours 55 minutes
   c 3 hours

7. On train 647, how long is the ride from New York to Washington?
   a 3 hours 20 minutes
   b 2 hours 55 minutes
   c 3 hours

Train Timetable

TRAIN NAME		Metroliner Service	Charter Oak	Metroliner Service
TRAIN NUMBER		125	647	127
DAYS OF OPERATION		Daily ExSa	Daily	Daily ExFrSu
TRAIN SERVICE		R ✪ ☕ ☎	☕	R ✪ ☕ ☎
New York, NY	Dp	6 00P	6 30P	7 00P
Newark, NJ	↓	R 6 13P	6 44P	R 7 13P
Metropark, NJ			6 59P	R 7 28P
Trenton, NJ	↓		7 22P	
Philadelphia, PA	Ar			
Philadelphia, PA	Dp	7 11P	7 53P	8 16P
Wilmington, DE	↓	7 31P	8 17P	8 36P
Baltimore, MD		8 14P	9 05P	9 19P
New Carrollton, MD	↓	D 8 41P	9 33P	D 9 46P
Washington, DC	Ar	8 55P	9 50P	9 55P

Legend:
   R   Stops only to receive passengers
   D   Stops only to discharge passengers
   R   All reserved train
   ☎   Railfone public telephone service
   ✪   Club Service
   ☕   Sandwiches, snack and beverage service

8. Refer to the schedule above. Complete the note below to make the instructions accurate.

Tim:
Loretta will meet us in Trenton around 7:30 p.m. So we'll have to get the train from New York that leaves at _____.
        6:00 P   6:30 P   7:00 P

That train's number is _____.
        125   647   127

The train trip lasts for about_____.
        ½ an hour   1 hour   3 hours

This train serves_____.
        no food   some snacks   full meals

11. Reading an Airline Schedule

Taking a trip by air? When you get to an airport, check inside for a TV display like the one below. The **departure** display will give you information about the plane you're taking. Notice the way the columns are arranged. You read **down** to find the time your plane is supposed to leave. Then you read **across** to get the latest information about that flight.

DEPARTURES

Scheduled Departure	Airline	Flight #	Destination	Gate	Status
9:30 A	Wings	234	Vieques	12A	On Time
10:00 A	Soar	1001	Trinidad	14C	On Time
10:30 A	WOW	70	Chicago	5B	Cancelled
12:15 P	Daring	1246	Hawaii	24D	One Hour Delay
12:20 P	Cheep	300	Podunk/Alfafa/Boring	31	On Time

Practice using the **departures** chart. Imagine you're headed for Trinidad on the 10 a.m. flight. What airline will you be using? What is your flight number? Is your flight on time, or is it delayed? What gate will your plane be leaving from? Discuss how the signs below can help you get to the right gate.

Gates 22–30	Gates 10–21	Gates 31–40

Words and Meanings

cancelled—called off; not going to happen

delay—not going to happen as scheduled; will happen later than planned

departure—leaving

destination—the place you're going to

schedule—a list of times

status—the latest information about the flight

Use the display chart on page 30 to answer questions 1–8.

1. You are flying to Hawaii. What airline are you taking?

   a Cheep
   b Soar
   c Daring

2. When you get to the airport, you see that your flight to Hawaii will

   a leave on time.
   b leave one hour late.
   c leave from Gate 5B.

3. You are flying to Vieques. Your plane will leave from Gate

   a 930.   b 234.   c 12A.

4. Circle the sign you will follow to get to the gate for your trip to Vieques.

   a Gates 22–30   b Gates 10–21 c Gates 31–40

5. If you are flying to Boring, what airline will you take?

   a Cheep
   b WOW
   c Soar

6. Flight 300 makes

   a one stop.
   b two stops.
   c three stops.

7. Which flight has been called off, or cancelled?
   a #70   b #1001   c #1246

8. Most airlines ask you to check in **one hour** before the scheduled departure time. What time should you check in for your flight to Alfafa?

   a at 12 p.m.
   b at 11:20 a.m.
   c at 1:20 p.m.

Answer questions 9 and 10 on your own. Then discuss your answers.

9. When you check in at an airport, you will be asked for a **Photo ID**. What do you think a Photo ID is?

   a A camera that you're carrying to take photos on your trip.
   b A ticket that shows you have a reservation on the plane.
   c A form of identification—like a driver's license—that shows a picture of you.

10. If your flight has been cancelled—like flight 70 to Chicago—what's the best thing to do?

    a Go home and plan another trip.
    b Go to the airline desk and ask to be put on another flight.
    c Wait at the gate where you were supposed to board.

Vocabulary

Choose the best meaning for the word or words in dark letters. Circle your answer.

1. A **schedule** tells about
   a interesting *places.*
   b *times* for doing things.
   c *word meanings.*

2. **Frequency** means
   a *when*, or *how often.*
   b *go back*, or *leave.*
   c *where* or *what.*

3. On a train schedule, **Departs** means
   a the train *goes* to this place.
   b you must *get off* the train.
   c the train *leaves* at this time.

4. On a train schedule, **Arrives** means
   a the time you should get to the station to catch the train.
   b the time the train stops at certain places on its route.
   c the time a train will get to a destination.

5. On a train schedule, **Discharge** means
   a let passengers *off* the train.
   b *return* to the place the train started.
   c let new passengers *get on* the train.

6. A **bus schedule** tells you
   a when the bus leaves from one place and arrives at another place.
   b how to get to the bus station and find the departure gate.
   c how much you will have to pay to get from one place to another.

7. Who must **yield**? Study the picture. Circle the best answer.

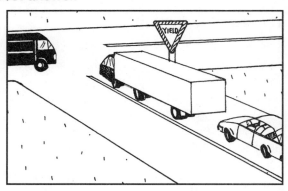

   a the van at the left
   b just the truck
   c the truck and the car

8. In this picture the police have stopped a car. What was the driver most likely doing wrong?

   a Passing in a no-passing area.
   b Driving at 50 miles an hour.
   c Driving at 25 miles an hour.

Comprehension

Choose the best meaning for the word or words in dark letters. Circle your answers.

CENTERVILLE TO OAK HILL MONDAY–FRIDAY, EXCEPT HOLIDAYS			
Leave	Arrive	Leave	Arrive
AM	AM	PM	PM
12:30L	1:07	4:00E	4:31
6:00L	6:37	X4:46E	5:17
6:53L	7:30	5:28E	5:58
7:56L	8:33	6:07E	6:38
9:00E	9:31	6:36L	7:13
10:00E	10:31	7:00E	7:31
11:00E	11:31	8:00E	8:37
12:00E	12:31	9:00E	9:31
1:00E	1:31	10:00E	10:31
2:00E	2:31	11:00E	11:31
3:00L	3:37	PM	PM
PM	PM		

Shaded area indicates rush hour.

L—Local train
E—Express train
X—Does not stop at Elm Street

Use the schedule above to answer questions 1–5.

1. Look at the key at the bottom of the schedule. Find **E**. The earliest **express** train from Centerville to Oak Hill leaves Centerville at

   a 1:00 p.m. b 7:56 a.m. c 9:00 a.m.

2. What does the shaded part of the schedule tell you about?

   a trains that run during rush hour
   b trains that don't stop at Elm Street
   c trains that run only on Holidays

3. A **local train** stops at many places. Which of the following is a local?

   a the 2:00 p.m. b the 3:00 p.m. c the 6:07 a.m.

4. What does the **X** mean in **X4:46E**?

   a This train has been cancelled.
   b not an express train
   c no Elm Street stop

5. You have an appointment in Oak Hill at 6:30 p.m. To get there in time, the latest train you can take from Centerville is the

   a 5:28 p.m.   b. 4:00 p.m.   c 6:36 p.m.

6. Look at each sign. Find its correct meaning in the box below. Write the meaning next to each sign.

_____

_____

_____

_____

_____

Slippery when wet
School children cross here
You can get gasoline here
Scenic route
Railroad crossing
No trucks allowed

READING AND MONEY

You can earn it. You can spend it. You can save it. What is IT? It's **money**, of course.

To use money **wisely**, you need to be a **sharp reader**. For example, you must read to find out:

- Is this sale really a good deal?

- What kind of jobs are being advertised? Which ones can I do? What will I earn?

- How can I keep track of my money so that I don't go into too much debt?

- How can I use bank accounts in a way that will help me?

In this section, you can apply your reading skills to help you spend, earn, and save in a sensible way.

Contents

A **sale** gives you a chance to buy things at a reduced price. Before you shop and buy, however, make sure you understand all the details in the sale announcement. This is called **"reading the fine print."**

Read the **advertisement** below and the notes that help you interpret it.

the store's name

MoneyMart's
Huge Winter Clearance Sale!

12:01 a.m. to 7:00 p.m. Saturday, April 9

the day and time of the sale

50% off All Items
listed below!

how much you can expect to save

Skis, sleds, and winter clothes

Start-up fireplace logs

Blarney's Soups and Waffle Mixes

Selected items from our Home Furnishing Department *

All lawn mowers and tractors **

Twit Birdseed ***

only the items in the list below are on sale

50% Off!

One Day Only!

* Does not include chairs, sofas, and beds
** Latest models not included in sale
*** 100-pound sacks only

an asterisk (*) means look for the matching asterisk (*) at the bottom of the ad to get more information

Use the ad on page 36 to answer questions 1–5.

1. Which things at MoneyMart are on sale?

   a everything in the store
   b only things to use in the winter
   c only things listed in the ad

2. The sale at MoneyMart is going on

   a for just a few hours.
   b all during April.
   c all day on Saturday, April 9.

3. According to the ad, if you want to buy a sofa at MoneyMart, you can

   a get it at 50% off the original price.
   b expect to pay full price for it.
   c select the sofa you want for a discount.

4. To take advantage of the Twit Birdseed sale, you'll have to buy

   a a 100-pound sack.
   b a 20-pound sack.
   c two 50-pound sacks.

5. You want to buy a lawn mower at MoneyMart. To get one on sale, you'll

   a buy the latest model.
   b send in a coupon to get a partial refund.
   c buy last-year's model.

Study the ad below. Answer the questions about it.

FRISKYOU MOTORS

☆ GRAND OPENING SALE: ☆
OFFERS GOOD JUNE AND JULY

To welcome our new customers, we offer the following FREE services:

• FREE car inspection! *
• FREE tune-up!**
• FREE oil change! (Tues.-Thurs. only)
• FREE car wash! (Tues.-Thurs. only)

* Free inspection does not include labor.
** Does not include labor. Tune-up not available for SUVs, trucks, or pre-1998 cars.

6. Which of these services is really **"free"**?

   a the car wash
   b the inspection
   c the tune-up on a 1995 Chevy

7. The Grand Opening sale is *over* at the end of the day on:

   a June 30.
   b July 31.
   c August 1.

8. You can get a free oil-change if you bring your car in on a

   a Monday.
   b Sunday.
   c Wednesday.

9. Which vehicle **cannot** get a tune-up at the sale?

   a a 2000 Mustang convertible
   b a 2001 Land Rover SUV
   c a 1998 Honda sedan

2. More About Sales

As you read the poster at left, you can **figure out** that:

- **Selected** means only **certain** items are on sale.

- **Up to** means that **some** items are reduced by 50%. Other items may not be reduced that much.

When there's a big sale at a store, you'll find that price tags on the items may tell you:

- The original price (usually with a line through it).

- The sale price.

Sometimes there's even a line through the sale price, with a further reduction below it! 50%, as advertised on the poster, means half. Half of $100 (the original price of the sweater in the example tag below) is $50. So, you can see that the sweater is not really selling for half price. In fact, at $80, it's selling for $30 more than "half price." It helps to do a little arithmetic when you're sale shopping!

Of course, it's your decision to buy or not to buy after you figure out whether the sale price is really great— and whether you really need the item on sale.

Original Price
$100.00

Sale Price
$80.00

Additional Reduction
$10.00

Words and Meanings

original price—what the item first sold for in the store

sale—a reduction, or lowering, of the original price

selected items—just *some* things that are chosen to be on sale

up to—the greatest but not only reduction you'll find on some items in the store

1. Read across each row to find the original price, the % off at the sale, and the sale price. Then figure out how much money you will save on the item. Write the amount saved in the far right column.

Original Price	% Off	Sale Price	Amount Saved
$14.99	15%	$12.74	$2.25
$48.00	15%	$40.80	
$69.00	15%	$58.65	
$32.00	20%	$25.60	
$59.88	15%	$50.90	
$8.00	20%	$6.40	

Refer to this ad to answer questions 2–5. Circle the correct answers.

THE MEN'S STORE

HALF PRICE
Men's short-sleeve knit shirt closeout

• Full button-front 100% polyester
• Colors: blue, yellow, green*
• Sizes: S, M, L, and XL

WAS: $25.00
NOW: $12.50

SAVE 20%**
Men's casual slacks***

* Not all colors in all sizes
** Cashier will deduct from ticketed price.
*** Sizes 38–44

2. The Men's Store offers 20% savings on:
   a all men's casual slacks.
   b only slacks sizes 38–44.
   c men's slacks and short-sleeve shirts.

3. In the ad, the words **short-sleeve knit shirt closeout** mean:
   a only shirts with closed collars are on sale.
   b these shirts may not be in the store again.
   c the shirts are damaged in some way.

4. A yellow shirt:
   a is sure to be available in S, M, L, and XL sizes.
   b may be available in sizes 38 to 44 only.
   c may not be available in the size you wear.

5. The ticket on the casual slacks will:
   a show the original price.
   b show the sale price.
   c say **Save 20%.**

3. Unit Price

When shopping at a supermarket, you've probably seen Unit Price labels like the one below on various items. **Unit price** means **the price per ounce** or **the price per pound** of an item. Below is an example of a Unit Price label.

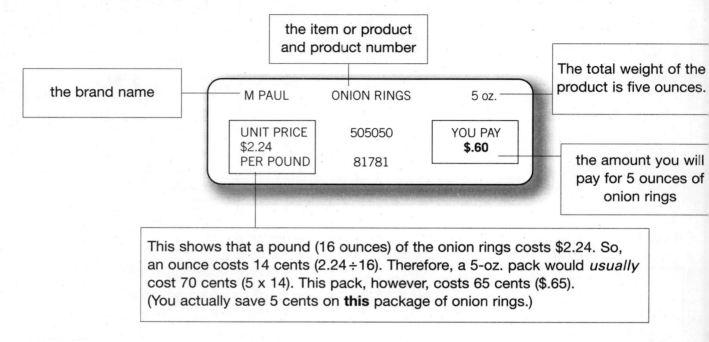

the item or product and product number

the brand name

The total weight of the product is five ounces.

M PAUL   ONION RINGS   5 oz.

UNIT PRICE $2.24 PER POUND   505050   81781   YOU PAY **$.60**

the amount you will pay for 5 ounces of onion rings

This shows that a pound (16 ounces) of the onion rings costs $2.24. So, an ounce costs 14 cents (2.24 ÷ 16). Therefore, a 5-oz. pack would *usually* cost 70 cents (5 x 14). This pack, however, costs 65 cents ($.65). (You actually save 5 cents on **this** package of onion rings.)

Doing the numbers isn't always easy. But you should learn how to read labels, like the one above, on products that you often buy. In the long run, you can save money by figuring out whether what you pay is a real reduction in price. For example, a label like this would show that you are not getting a reduction:

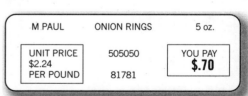

M PAUL   ONION RINGS   5 oz.

UNIT PRICE $2.24 PER POUND   505050   81781   YOU PAY **$.70**

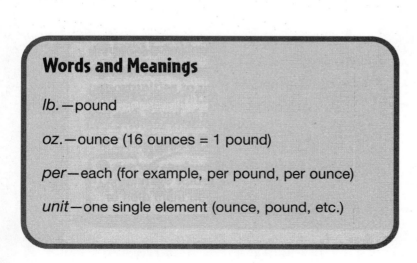

Words and Meanings

lb. —pound

oz. —ounce (16 ounces = 1 pound)

per —each (for example, per pound, per ounce)

unit —one single element (ounce, pound, etc.)

1. Which item below weighs the most?

   a

M PAUL	FISH CAKES	8 oz.
UNIT PRICE $1.80 PER POUND	505050 81881	YOU PAY $.90

   b

M PAUL	DRIED YAMS	12 oz.
UNIT PRICE $1.20 PER POUND	505050 81781	YOU PAY $.90

   c

M PAUL	SHRIMP CAKES	5 oz.
UNIT PRICE $4.40 PER POUND	505050 81781	YOU PAY $1.65

2. You want to buy a pack of onion rings. The pack has this label:

M PAUL	ONION RINGS	5 oz.
UNIT PRICE $2.24 PER POUND	505050 81781	YOU PAY $.65

   The store also sells a 15-oz. pack for $1.60. If you buy the 15-oz. pack instead of the 5-oz. pack, you will

   a get more onion rings for your money.
   b get fewer onion rings for your money.
   c pay the same for the number of onion rings.

Use the picture below to help you answer questions 3–6.

3. What will you pay for **two pounds** of onions?
   a $2.99   **b** $5.98   **c** $6.00

4. How much does **one bag** of potatoes cost?
   a $2.99   **b** $3.99   **c** $1.29

5. **Three bunches** of broccoli will cost
   a $1.29.   **b** $2.58.   **c** $3.87.

6. For **eight oranges**, you'll pay
   a $1.00.   **b** $3.00.   **c** $2.00.

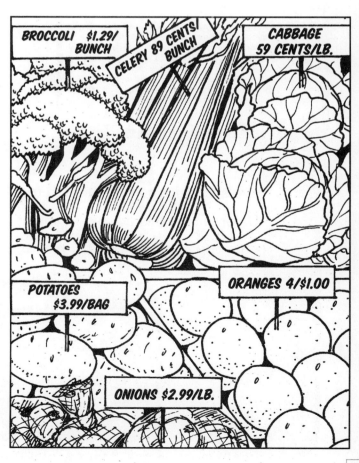

4. Offers in the Mail

Most of us get lots of tempting **"free"** offers in the mail. Very few offers are really "free." Don't say yes unless you've read and understood the fine print. Read the offer below as an example.

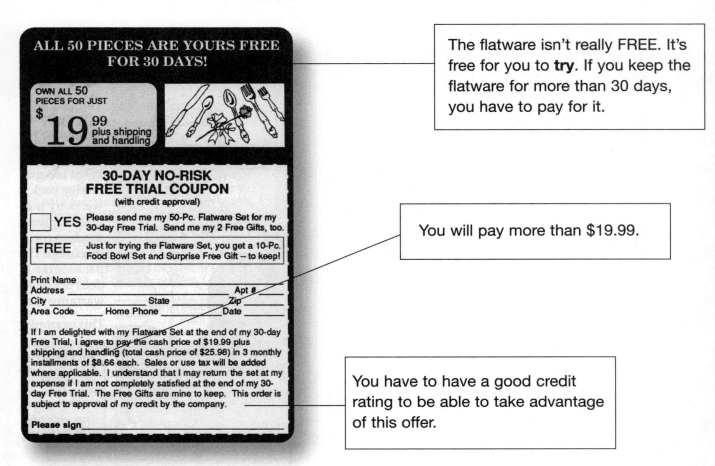

ALL 50 PIECES ARE YOURS FREE FOR 30 DAYS!

OWN ALL 50 PIECES FOR JUST
$19.99 plus shipping and handling

30-DAY NO-RISK FREE TRIAL COUPON
(with credit approval)

[ ] **YES** Please send me my 50-Pc. Flatware Set for my 30-day Free Trial. Send me my 2 Free Gifts, too.

FREE Just for trying the Flatware Set, you get a 10-Pc. Food Bowl Set and Surprise Free Gift — to keep!

Print Name _____
Address _____ Apt # _____
City _____ State _____ Zip _____
Area Code _____ Home Phone _____ Date _____

If I am delighted with my Flatware Set at the end of my 30-day Free Trial, I agree to pay the cash price of $19.99 plus shipping and handling (total cash price of $25.98) in 3 monthly installments of $8.66 each. Sales or use tax will be added where applicable. I understand that I may return the set at my expense if I am not completely satisfied at the end of my 30-day Free Trial. The Free Gifts are mine to keep. This order is subject to approval of my credit by the company.

Please sign_____

> The flatware isn't really FREE. It's free for you to **try**. If you keep the flatware for more than 30 days, you have to pay for it.

> You will pay more than $19.99.

> You have to have a good credit rating to be able to take advantage of this offer.

Here's a tip for sorting through the fliers and ads you get in the mail—Ask yourself: "Before I saw this ad, did I think at all about buying a product like this?" If the answer is no, you should promptly throw out the ad.

Words and Meanings

credit approval—You can't get the items unless your credit card company states that you pay your bills on time.

free trial—trying out the product with no cost to you

shipping and handling—what the manufacturer charges you for packing and mailing the item to you

1. **Read the offer carefully. Write the captions below on the lines where they belong.**

ALL 50 PIECES ARE YOURS FREE FOR 30 DAYS!

OWN ALL 50 PIECES FOR JUST
$ **19** 99 plus shipping and handling

30-DAY NO-RISK FREE TRIAL COUPON
(with credit approval)

YES Please send me my 50-Pc. Flatware Set for my 30-day Free Trial. Send me my 2 Free Gifts, too.

FREE Just for trying the Flatware Set, you get a 10-Pc. Food Bowl Set and Surprise Free Gift – to keep!

Print Name _____
Address _____ Apt # _____
City _____ State _____ Zip _____
Area Code _____ Home Phone _____ Date _____

If I am delighted with my Flatware Set at the end of my 30-day Free Trial, I agree to pay the cash price of $19.99 plus shipping and handling (total cash price of $25.98) in 3 monthly installments of $8.66 each. Sales or use tax will be added where applicable. I understand that I may return the set at my expense if I am not completely satisfied at the end of my 30-day Free Trial. The Free Gifts are mine to keep. This order is subject to approval of my credit by the company.

Please sign_____

a. _____

b. _____

c. _____

d. _____

e. _____

- You can keep these even if you decide to return the flatware set.
- Check here if you accept this offer.
- If you send the flatware back, you pay the postage.

- If you keep the set, you may also have to pay a sales tax.
- This is what you'll pay altogether if you decide to keep the flatware.

Write your answers to questions 2–5 on the lines below.

2. Would **you** order the flatware set described in the mail offer above? Explain why or why not.

_____
_____
_____

3. Write about a mail offer you've received. What was the offer?

_____
_____

4. Did you order it? _____

5. Why or why not? _____
_____
_____

5. Ordering From a Catalog

Many stores send out **catalogs**. By using a catalog, you can order items by mail, over the telephone, or through the store's Web site. The catalog describes each item, tells its price, and usually gives a number for the item, such as #06A312. Inside the catalog, you'll find an **order form** like the one below. To be sure to get the item you want, you have to fill out the form correctly.

Write the correct number (given in the catalog) for the item you want to order. You may not get what you want if you give the wrong item number from the catalog.

the price of each item

name of item

how many of each item you want

the amount you get by multiplying the quantity by the unit price

Item #	Description	Color	Size	Qty.	Unit Price	Total

Put a check in the box near the words that say how you want to pay for your order.

☐ Charge my Visa/MasterCard

☐ Check or MO enclosed
(DO NOT enclose CASH)

Subtotal	
If delivered in city, add 5% sales tax	
Total	

Trail Blazers. Comfortable, long-lasting, waterproof! Colors: Black or Brown. Sizes 4-12 (no half-sizes). $44.00   #421B113

Snow Cap. Flaps protect your ears in the coldest weather! Colors: Black, Brown, Gray, Red. One size fits all. $12.98   #221C214

Snuggle-In Jacket. Fully lined. Colors: Sun-glow, Sky-Gray, Snow-White. Sizes S, M, L, XL. $51.00   #321A114

Words and Meanings

catalog—a book containing pictures of items for sale, along with information about the items

charge—to put the cost on your credit card instead of paying cash right away

MO—money order

Qty.—quantity (how many)

subtotal—what the prices add up to before you add sales tax

1. Refer to the catalog descriptions on page 44. Fill in the order form below to order one each of all three items. To start you off, the information about the hiking boots is already filled in.

Item #	Description	Color	Size	Qty.	Unit Price	Total
#421B113	Trail Blazers	Brown	12	1	$44.00	$44.00

☐ Charge my Visa/MasterCard

☐ Check or MO enclosed
(DO NOT enclose CASH)

Subtotal	
If delivered in city, add 5% sales tax	
Total	

2. **Use the picture and information below to fill out the order form.**

Fill in the form to order:

- 1 yellow **BetterSweater** in size 8.
- 2 pairs of **Listen-Up Earmuffs**

You want all these things *sent to* Ellen Ramirez, P.O. Box #52, Benson, Arizona, 85602.

You are enclosing an MO (money order), so you won't have to fill in the CHARGE TO section. You **do** want the package gift-wrapped.

BetterSweater

Just the thing for special occasions!
Colors: Red, Yellow, Green, Black.
Sizes 4–16.
$16.50   #738C12

Listen-Up Earmuffs

Brown only. One size fits all.
$8.50   #738D14

$\mathcal{Z}$-$\mathcal{L}$ DEPARTMENT STORE

Please use this coupon for mail orders.

Date _____

Item #	Description & Color	Size	Qty.	Unit Price	Total

☐ Charge my Visa/MasterCard

☐ Check or MO enclosed
(DO NOT enclose CASH)

☐ Gift Wrap

Subtotal	
If delivered in city, add 5% sales tax	
TOTAL	

CHARGE TO:

Visa/MasterCard _____

Name _____

Address _____

City/State/Zip _____

SEND TO:

Name _____

Address _____

City/State/Zip _____

SATISFACTION GUARANTEED OR YOUR MONEY BACK.

6. Classified Ads

The **Classified Ads** *(advertisements)* section of a newspaper tells about homes and many other things that are for rent or sale. Many classified ads give a very short description, and use lots of **abbreviations**, or *short ways of naming things*. To understand the ads, you have to figure out the abbreviations. Below are examples of three classified ads you might find.

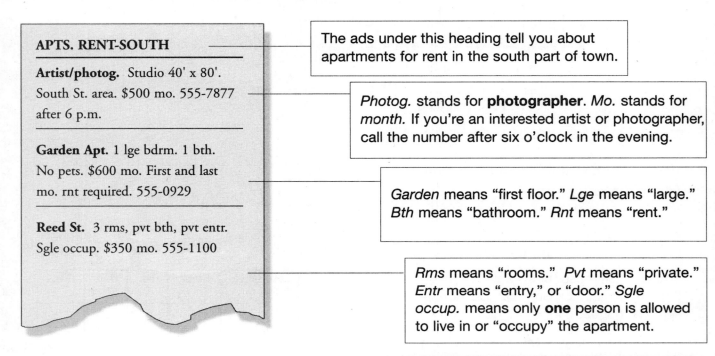

APTS. RENT-SOUTH

Artist/photog. Studio 40' x 80'. South St. area. $500 mo. 555-7877 after 6 p.m.

Garden Apt. 1 lge bdrm. 1 bth. No pets. $600 mo. First and last mo. rnt required. 555-0929

Reed St. 3 rms, pvt bth, pvt entr. Sgle occup. $350 mo. 555-1100

The ads under this heading tell you about apartments for rent in the south part of town.

Photog. stands for **photographer**. *Mo.* stands for *month*. If you're an interested artist or photographer, call the number after six o'clock in the evening.

Garden means "first floor." *Lge* means "large." *Bth* means "bathroom." *Rnt* means "rent."

Rms means "rooms." *Pvt* means "private." *Entr* means "entry," or "door." *Sgle occup.* means only **one** person is allowed to live in or "occupy" the apartment.

Abbreviations vary from time to time, from ad to ad, and from newspaper to newspaper. Use your apartment-hunting sleuth skills to figure out what the abbreviations mean. Other abbreviations you might find in classified ads are listed in Words and meanings, right.

Words and Meanings

eff—(efficiency) a one-room apartment with a kitchen and a bathroom

flr—floor

furn—furnished

kit—kitchen

lr—living room

refs req—information about you from people who know you well, such as an employer

util—utilities, such as electricity or gas or oil heat

vic.—vicinity, or what it's near

yd—yard

w/w—wall-to-wall, as carpeting

Test your skills for figuring out abbreviations. Find the answers to questions 1–6 by studying the classified ad on this page.

CLASSIFIED

Apartments for Rent
South, Furnished

Broad & Snyder Near Bennet Elem. Sch. 5 rms, 2 bth. $1200 mo., incl. util. After 5 pm. 555-0678

Broad nr Wolf Beautiful mod 2rms, 1 bth. $950 mo. A/C. Utils not incl. Call super. 555-9454

Modern 1 bdrm Small but sweet: lr, kit, tile bth, new decoration, w/w carp, A/C. $850 mo., plus util. No pets. Refs req. 555-7077

15th & Snyder 1st flr. 1 lge rm (50 x 50) + bth. Beautiful furn. $800 mo. plus util. Refs req + fst/l mo. rent. 555-9733 bet. 6–9 pm.

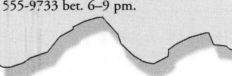

1. All the apartments in the ad

   a already have furniture in them.
   b allow dogs and cats.
   c would be comfortable for a family of six.

2. As a renter, you would have to pay for utilities in

   a two of the apartments.
   b all of the apartments.
   c three of the apartments.

3. You would have to supply references to prove you are a good tenant if you wanted to rent the

   a modern 1 bdrm.
   b apartment at Broad near Wolf.
   c apartment at Broad & Snyder.

4. In the ads, what do you think A/C means?

   a all Clothes
   b after Christmas
   c air Conditioning

5. **fst/l** means **first** and **last**. If you want the apartment at 15th and Snyder, you will have to give the landlord

   a $50.
   b $800.
   c $1,600.

6. You want the apartment at Broad nr (near) Wolf. To inquire about it, call

   a after 5 p.m.
   b the superintendent.
   c between 6 and 9 p.m.

7. Using Classified Ads to Look for a Job

Are you looking for a job you **like** and **can do**? One place to look is in the **Help Wanted** section of the Classified Ads section of your newspaper. Like all classified ads, these help-wanted ads are short, and often use abbreviations. You have to read them carefully to figure out whether or not to apply for the position.

> This might be a good job if you couldn't work all day long, Monday through Friday.

> You probably have to take a test to see if you qualify for this job.

> Notice the abbreviations. Here, **Exp** means **experience**, and **refs** means **references**.

HELP WANTED

Assistant, Part-time, for small music School in Wallcreek. 15–20 hours per week. Must have excellent phone, typing, and bookkeeping skills. Responsibility is to keep records up to date. Exp a must! Provide refs. $8/hr! 555-7773.

Clerical Position available in dentist's office. Must have experience in health insurance and have computer skills. $8–$10/hr. Call Healing Arts Center, 555-6045.

Data Entry Operators: Moderate speed with above-average accuracy. Monday–Friday work week. Flexible hours, full-time or part-time, day or evening hours. $8.25/hour. Benefits: enrollment for health, dental after 30 days. Free training available for qualified applicants. For appt or more info, call 888-555-1010.

Groovy Rustic Lodge, 35 min. west of Watertown, seeks responsible employees: Kitchen/Dishwasher, Service/Wait staff, Maintenance/Grounds. Seasonal. Must have car. Call Pete at 555-5117.

> Your pay would be somewhere between these amounts, depending on your experience.

> **Seasonal** means just for part of the year.

> Notice that the ad doesn't say how much the different jobs pay.

Words and Meanings

appt—appointment

benefits—special payments or extras you get in addition to a salary

flexible—able to be changed or adjusted

pref—preferred, not always required

references (or refs)—letters from people you've worked for, telling about your skills and work habits

resume—written information *you* supply about other jobs you've had, and about your education

Refer to the help wanted ads on this page to find the answers to questions 1–8. Circle the answers you choose.

1. Which job is for part-time **only**?

   a (2) **b** (6) **c** (5)

2. For which job **must** you have a car?

   a (1) **b** (3) **c** (5)

3. Which job offers **benefits**?

   a (3) **b** (4) **c** (1)

4. The salary at Toon's Music Store is based on your

   a experience.
   b ability to play the guitar.
   c knowledge of computers.

5. The job advertised in (3) pays how much per hour?

   a $11 **b** $30 **c** $10

6. The job advertised in (2) **doesn't** tell you

   a how to apply.
   b what phone number you should call.
   c what the salary is.

7. In ad (6), **flexible hrs** means that you:

   a can work only during the morning.
   b may change your work schedule now and then.
   c must be in the office at least part of each day.

8. To apply for classified job (1), you should

   a go to the store and ask about the job.
   b call the store and ask for an appointment.
   c bring along a musical instrument.

CLASSIFIED

Help Wanted

(1) Assistant Manager for music store. Must have strong knowledge of guitar and electric accessories. Should be efficient and cheerful. Salary according to experience. Apply in person, 9–5, Toon's Music Store, Valley Mall. No phone calls.

(2) Daytime Cook Wanted. Full- or part-time. Call or apply in person. P & G Restaurant, 555-9000.

(3) Doctors' Office needs receptionist. Must have computer skills, great phone voice. 30 hrs a week: $330. 128 Main Street, Newbery. Call Jill, 555-9876, for appt.

(4) Food Market Manager. Must have experience. Top wages, all benefits, plus bonus. 7315 Woodland Ave., Westbery. Call between 9 a.m.–1 p.m. to set up appointment. 555-FOOD.

(5) Full- or Part-time Nanny, in our home, for twin girls, age 4. Reliable and energetic. Must have references, driver's license, and own car. $12/hr. Call 555-1438 between 6 p.m. and 10 p.m.

(6) General Office Work: Part-time, with flexible hrs, in Oldbery area. Filing, computer word processing. $8.50/hr. 555-2950 Mon.–Wed.

9. Which one of the jobs above would you apply for?

   _____

   On the lines below, explain.

   _____

   _____

   _____

   _____

Vocabulary

Choose the best meaning for the word or words in dark letters. Circle your answers.

1. At a sale, **original price** means
   a what the item costs now.
   b what the item first cost.
   c how much you can expect to save.

2. In an ad, **Up to 80% Off** means
   a some items are reduced by 80%.
   b all items are reduced by 80%.
   c everything in the store is on sale.

3. **Plus shipping and handling** means
   a you will pay the cost of packing and mailing the item.
   b the store will pay the packing and mailing cost.
   c the price of the item includes packing and mailing it.

4. **Free trial** means
   a the item is yours to keep whether you like it or not.
   b you can send the item back at any time you like.
   c you can try the item free for a certain number of days.

5. In a help wanted ad, **flexible hours** means
   a the job is only a part-time one.
   b you will work only when you feel like it.
   c your work time may change from day to day.

Find the abbreviations in the box that stand for the words listed below it. Write the abbreviation on the correct line. (You will use all but one of the abbreviations.)

lb.	oz.	MO
qty	yd	lr
util	vic.	ea.
furn	flr	bth

6. yard _____

7. pound _____

8. furnished _____

9. quantity _____

10. floor _____

11. ounces _____

12. money order _____

13. utilities _____

14. each _____

15. living room _____

16. bath _____

Comprehension

Use this supermarket ad to answer questions 1–5.

Fang Dog Food! 12 cans $10.00.
Original price: 90 cents per can

Mom's Chicken Soup!
Buy 8 $2.00 cans,
Get a 9th can free!
(with coupon)

Delicious Oranges!
One pound $4.00.
Two pounds for
just $8.00!

Flarthers Floor Wax.
Original price: $7.50 per can.
Now $7.00 per can with purchase of five
cans. (Write to Flarthers for refund.
Include bill-of-sale and label from each can.)

Circle the correct answers.

1. Which items are **not** on sale?

   a oranges   **b** floor wax   **c** chicken soup

2. If you buy 12 cans of Fang Dog Food, you'll save

   a 80 cents.   **b** Nothing.   **c** 90 cents.

3. To take advantage of the floor wax sale, you have to

   a bring in a coupon.
   b write to Flarthers.
   c buy just one can.

4. How much does **one** can of Mom's Chicken Soup cost?

   a 80 cents   **b** 90 cents   **c** $2.00

5. If you get to the check-out counter with **9 cans** of Mom's Chicken Soup, you will be charged

   a $18.00.   **b** $19.00.   **c** $16.00.

Read the help wanted ad below to answer questions 6–9.

Caretaker needed. Part-time residents need reliable person to care for home. Oct.–Apr., Mon.–Fri. only. Must have references. Possible lodging Mon.–Thurs. 1 pers. only. No pets allowed. Call 212-555-5550, 6–10 p.m. Mon.–Thurs. Salary negotiable.

6. Could you live in this house all year?

   _____

   How do you know? _____

   _____

7. If you got this job, what do you think your responsibilities would be?

   _____

   _____

   _____

8. What do you think **salary negotiable** means?

   _____

   _____

   _____

   _____

9. Who would be best suited for the job described in the ad?

   a a person who needs a winter home for every day of the week
   b a person who has another place to live on weekends
   c a person who has two kids and some pets to care for at home

8. A Checking Account

If you have a **checking account**, that means the bank will let you **deposit** (put) money *into* your account, and also **withdraw** (take out) money *from* your account by writing a check. Keeping a record of your checking account is very important.

At right is an example of a filled-out **deposit** slip (a form to use when you're *putting money into* your checking account).

Below is an example of a **check** that Stella Uribe **paid** to M. Scott and Son, meaning that she **withdrew** money from her checking account.

DEPOSIT SLIP

Nickle Bank and Trust Co.

Date _Jan. 12 2002_

Checking Account # _72564_

Name _Stella Uribe_

		Dollars	Cents
Cash		100	00
Checks	1	50	00
	2	35	50
	3		
	4		
Bank Use only	5		
	Total	185	50

No. 291
April 7 2002
To *M. Scott and Son*
For *Paint Bill*

Bal Fwd	$189.60
Amt Deposited	10.00
Total	199.60
Amt This Check	5.63
Bal	$193.97

Stella Uribe   No. 291

April 7   20 _02_

Pay to the order of _M. Scott and Son_ $ 5.63

five and _____ ⁶³⁄₁₀₀   Dollars

Nickle Bank and Trust Co.
Main Street

memo _paint bill_   _Stella Uribe_

0291:027::091:447259

This is the check stub that Stella keeps for her own records.

Words and Meanings

balance (or bal)—how much money you have in your bank account

bank account—money you have in a bank

deposit—to put money into your bank account

withdraw—to take money out of your bank account

Look at the check and check stub on page 52 to answer questions 1–5. Circle the answers you choose.

1. On the check stub, **No. 291** is

   a the number of the check.
   b the amount the check is made out for.
   c the number of the bank.

2. On the check stub, **To** means

   a for what the money was paid.
   b to whom the money was paid.
   c the date the check was written.

3. *Before* she wrote the check to M. Scott and Son, Stella had $189.60 in her checking account. This amount is shown on the check stub line that means:

   a balance.
   b amount of this check.
   c balance brought forward.

4. Where does Stella write what she wrote the check for?

   a on the check and the check stub
   b only on the stub
   c only after **memo** on the check

5. After Stella writes the check to M. Scott and Son, how much does she have left in her checking account?

   a $193.97   b $5.63   c $189.60

6. Fill in the deposit slip below. Here is the information you need:

   - On April 10, 2002, Stella Uribe deposited money at the bank.
   - Stella's account number is 72664.
   - Stella deposited $50.00 in cash.
   - She also deposited two checks. Check 1 was for $25.60. Check 2 was for $100.00.
   - Fill out the **Total** line on the deposit slip. To do this correctly, you will have to add up the numbers under *Cash* and *Checks*.

DEPOSIT SLIP

Nickle Bank and Trust Co.

Date _____

Checking Account # _____

Name _____

		Dollars	Cents
Cash			
Checks	1		
	2		
	3		
	4		
Bank Use only	5		
	Total		

9. A Credit Card

The first thing to know about a credit card is that it doesn't **give** you money. The card **lends** you money, or allows you to **borrow** money. Here are some guidelines:

- You have to pay back the money you've borrowed.

- If you don't pay back **all** that you've borrowed, the credit card company will add a **finance charge**, or **interest**, to your next bill.

- The finance charge is usually a lot of money. It may add anywhere from **18% to 22%** to the total of what you've borrowed. The finance charge is how credit card companies make money. So, the credit card company is hoping that you *won't* pay off all of your bill at the end of the month. If you only pay the minimum due each month, you will end up paying much more for the item than it originally cost.

Here's a typical credit card statement to someone who paid his or her *previous* bill on time and in full:

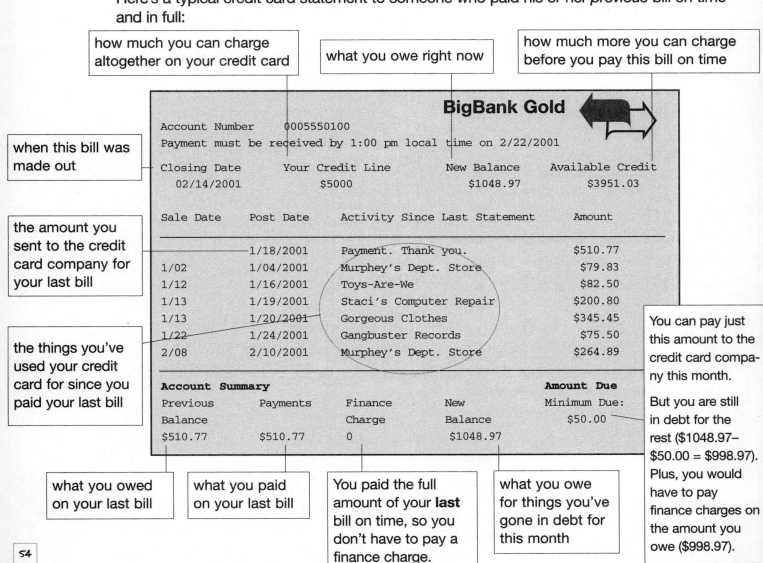

how much you can charge altogether on your credit card

what you owe right now

how much more you can charge before you pay this bill on time

when this bill was made out

the amount you sent to the credit card company for your last bill

the things you've used your credit card for since you paid your last bill

BigBank Gold

Account Number   0005550100
Payment must be received by 1:00 pm local time on 2/22/2001

Closing Date	Your Credit Line	New Balance	Available Credit
02/14/2001	$5000	$1048.97	$3951.03

Sale Date	Post Date	Activity Since Last Statement	Amount
	1/18/2001	Payment. Thank you.	$510.77
1/02	1/04/2001	Murphey's Dept. Store	$79.83
1/12	1/16/2001	Toys-Are-We	$82.50
1/13	1/19/2001	Staci's Computer Repair	$200.80
1/13	1/20/2001	Gorgeous Clothes	$345.45
1/22	1/24/2001	Gangbuster Records	$75.50
2/08	2/10/2001	Murphey's Dept. Store	$264.89

Account Summary **Amount Due**

Previous Balance	Payments	Finance Charge	New Balance	Minimum Due:
$510.77	$510.77	0	$1048.97	$50.00

You can pay just this amount to the credit card company this month.

But you are still in debt for the rest ($1048.97–$50.00 = $998.97). Plus, you would have to pay finance charges on the amount you owe ($998.97).

what you owed on your last bill

what you paid on your last bill

You paid the full amount of your **last** bill on time, so you don't have to pay a finance charge.

what you owe for things you've gone in debt for this month

1. A credit card is a convenient way to

   a earn money.
   b get out of paying bills.
   c borrow money.

2. You won't have to pay a *finance charge* if you

   a charge the full amount of your credit line.
   b pay all that you owe each month.
   c buy just the things that your family really needs.

3. The **Payment must be received by** line tells you

   a when the credit card company must get your payment in the mail.
   b how much you owe the credit card company.
   c the day and time when you must mail your payment to the company.

4. The **sale date** tells when you bought things. You bought things at Toys-Are-We on

   a January 16.
   b January 12.
   c February 14.

5. The **post date** tells when the store sent your credit card charge to the credit card company. Who sent two charges?

   a Gorgeous Clothes
   b Gangbuster Records
   c Murphey's Department Store

Suppose you didn't pay the full amount you owed on your last credit card statement. You only paid $50. Then the Account Summary at the bottom of the statement on p. 54 would look like this:

Account Summary					Amount Due
Previous Balance	Payments	Finance Charge	New Balance		Minimum due: $50.00
$510.77	$50.00	$8.27	$1518.01		

Rate Summary
Number Days 30
Annual Percentage Rate 18.900%

6. There is a *Finance Charge* on the summary above because

   a you did not pay the total amount you owed last month.
   b you bought more things this month.
   c you forgot to pay anything on your bill last month.

7. Subtract the *Finance Charge* above from the *Payments*. How much of your $50.00 actually went toward paying off your Previous Balance?

   a $8.27   b $41.73   c $50.00

8. The New Balance above is the total of

   a what you bought this month plus what you owe from last month.
   b the amount of credit you still have available.
   c the items you bought just this month.

10. A Debit Card

A **debit card** is like a credit card, and also like a checking account.

Many people feel that a debit card encourages them to keep better track of their money when they go shopping. Here's the way it works:

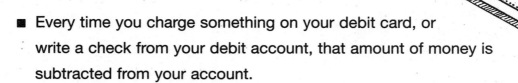

- You go to the bank and set up a **debit account.** You will get a debit account checkbook, and a debit card. You can use either one when you shop.

- You **deposit,** or **put into,** the bank as much money as you wish in your debit account.

- Every time you charge something on your debit card, or write a check from your debit account, that amount of money is subtracted from your account.

- You should keep a record of every purchase you make with your debit card. To see the total you've taken out of your account, you simply add up your charges.

- When your debit account balance is getting low, you should deposit more money into your account.

Keep these facts in mind:

- The bank charges a monthly fee for handling your debit account.

- It's up to **you** to keep track of how much you're spending from your account.

- If you run out of money in your debit account, the store will **not** accept your debit card or check.

1. With a debit account, you

   a pay all your bills at the end of the month.
   b are paying for things as you buy them.
   c use your credit card to buy things.

2. Suppose you deposit $300 in your debit account on the first of the month. The bank takes $6.00 of that for its monthly fee. What is your debit limit for the month?

   a $300.00   b $294.00   c $306.00

3. With a debit card

   a you are using money that you already have.
   b you are going into debt for money you will have to pay back.
   c you are borrowing money from the bank.

4. What's the **best** way to keep track of your debit account?

   a Wait for the bank to tell you how much you have in your account.
   b At the end of the month, write down all that you've charged to your account.
   c Keep a day-to-day list of the amount you've used from your account.

5. At the checkout counter, Sam gives the clerk his debit card. The clerk swipes the card through, then says, "Sorry, your debit card won't go through." This probably means that

   a there is something wrong with the store's debit card machine.
   b Sam should always use a credit card instead of a debit card.
   c Sam's debit account doesn't have enough money in it to pay for his purchases.

Write your answers to questions 6–8.

6. How is a debit card different from a credit card?

   _____
   _____
   _____
   _____
   _____

7. Would a debit account be a useful kind of account for **you**? Explain why or why not.

   _____
   _____
   _____
   _____
   _____
   _____
   _____

8. **Maxing out** means that you've used all of the money available in your debit account or money you can borrow on your credit card. On the lines below, write some advice you would give to someone who has maxed out.

   _____
   _____
   _____
   _____
   _____

11. A Savings Account

For money you want to save, you can open a **savings account** at the bank. Here are some advantages of a savings account:

■ The bank will pay you *interest* on the money you have in your savings account. This means that for every amount you put into your account and keep there for a while, the bank will *add* some money to it.

■ A savings account can keep you focused on big goals. You might be saving money so that you can take a great vacation, buy a house, or send your kids to college.

■ Most people who have a savings account are not as likely to dip into that account for day-to-day expenses. For that kind of thing, they'll try to use their cash, their debit or checking accounts, or credit cards.

Below is a bank **savings account statement** for Jorge. He has been saving money for quite a while. This year, Jorge couldn't put anything into his savings account. But he didn't take anything out of it, either!

YEAR-TO-DATE SUMMARY OF SAVINGS ACCOUNT

Beginning cash balance	$9,349. 63
Additions	0. 00
Interest	$485. 61
Subtractions	0. 00
Ending Cash Balance	$9,835.24

Total Value of Savings Account: $9,835.24

Words and Meanings

additions—the money you put into your bank account

cash balance—the money you have in your bank account

interest—the money the bank adds to your savings account

subtractions—the money you take out of your account

summary—a short way of giving information

Refer to the bank statement on page 58 to answer questions 1–5. Circle the answers you choose.

1. How much money did Jorge have in his savings account at the **beginning** of the year?

    a $9,835.24   b $485.61   c $9,349.63

2. The **Additions** line on the statement shows

    a what Jorge took *out* of his savings account.
    b how much money Jorge has left.
    c what Jorge put *into* his savings account.

3. Suppose Jorge had taken $100.00 out of his savings account. Where would this amount be shown?

    a after *Interest*
    b after *Subtractions*
    c after *Additions*

4. The amount after **Interest** shows

    a what Jorge owes the bank this year.
    b how much money Jorge's savings account earned this year.
    c how much money Jorge must deposit in his savings account.

5. How much does Jorge have in his savings account at the end of the year?

    a $9,835.24   b $485.61   c $9,329.63

Read questions 6 and 7. Write your answers on the lines below.

6. Suppose you have a savings account. Through the years, your account now adds up to $5,000. What are some ways you might use the money?

    _____
    _____
    _____
    _____
    _____

7. Jim has a savings account, a debit account, and a credit card.

    ■ He has $2,000.00 in his savings account.
    ■ He has $300.00 left on his debit card.
    ■ He can charge $500.00 more on his credit card.

    Jim wants to buy a used van that costs $2,000.

    a What are some ways that Jim could pay for the van?

    _____
    _____
    _____
    _____
    _____

    b Do you think Jim should buy the van?

    _____

    Explain why or why not.

    _____
    _____
    _____
    _____

A **budget** is a list or plan for how you will spend your money. A budget lists the **money that must go out,** and the **money that you expect to come in.** People keep budgets so that they can handle their money in a sensible way. Budgets can take different forms. But all good budgets, like the one below, list a person's "musts," or **out** payments, first. Then comes **in,** or what you expect to make during the month.

July Budget

Out:	Amount:
Rent	$550.00
Utilities	$ 52.00
Food	$375.00
Clothes	$ 40.00
Transportation	$120.00
Medical	$ 30.00
Credit Card Payments	$120.00 (approximate)
Total Out:	$1287.00
In:	
Jen's Salary	$600.50
Bart's Salary	$870.00
Rent from Tenant:	300.00
Medicaid Payment for Mom	$ 90.00
Total In:	$1860.50

The family budget above shows more money coming **in** than going **out.** However, sensible budgeters always know that there may be unexpected expenses that add to the money going out. They may choose to put any leftover money into a savings account.

1. The budget below is partly filled out. Use the following facts to fill in the rest of the budget and answer questions 2–5.

   ■ Louise and Lew pay $34.50 for utilities.

   ■ Their food bill is $450.00 a month.

   ■ In August, Louise and Lew spent $400.50 on clothes.

   ■ Their transportation to and around Canada will cost them $2,050.00

   ■ Louise and Lew had no medical expenses in August.

   ■ Louise makes $1,000.00 a month.

   ■ Lew also makes $1,000.00 a month.

   ■ Louise and Lew don't have a tenant right now.

August Budget	
Out	**Amount**
Rent	$600.00
Utilities	_____
Food	_____
Clothes	_____
Transportation	_____
Medical	_____
Credit Card Payments	$300.00
Total Out	_____
In:	
Louise's Salary	_____
Lew's Salary	_____
Rent from Tenant	_____
Total In	_____

2. **Out:** How much did Louise and Lew *spend* or *charge* in August? _____

3. **In:** How much did Louise and Lew *earn* together in August? _____

4. At the end of August, Louise and Lew spent more than they earned. How much more did they spend?

   a $1,835.00   b nothing   c $2,050.00

5. You may have some advice for Louise and Lew. If so, write your advice below.

   _____
   _____
   _____
   _____
   _____
   _____
   _____
   _____
   _____
   _____
   _____
   _____
   _____
   _____
   _____
   _____
   _____

Vocabulary

Choose the best meaning for the word or words in dark letters. Circle your answers.

1. A **deposit** is money that you
   a owe the bank.
   b take out of the bank.
   c put into the bank.

2. Your **bank balance** is
   a how much money you owe the bank.
   b how much money you have in the bank.
   c what the bank charges you for the checks you cash.

3. In an apartment-for-rent ad, **vic.** means
   a vacant.
   b in the vicinity of.
   c very nice.

4. Which abbreviation below means **each**?
   a ea.   b lb.   c oz.

5. A **finance charge** is what a credit card company
   a gives you when you pay your bill on time and in full.
   b subtracts from your bill.
   c charges you extra for what you still owe.

6. A **credit card** is a way of
   a borrowing money.
   b spending money you already have.
   c saving money for things you need.

7. In a savings account, **interest** is
   a what the bank charges you for having the account.
   b what you earn by keeping your money in the account.
   c your statement about why you are interested in starting the account.

8. A **debit card** allows you to
   a borrow money.
   b spend any amount of money you wish to spend.
   c use money that you've already put aside in the bank.

9. A **budget** helps you
   a earn more money.
   b spend more money.
   c plan how to use your money.

10. When you **withdraw** money, you are
   a taking money out of your bank account.
   b saving money in your savings account.
   c putting money into your bank account.

Comprehension

Read the ad carefully. Then answer the questions that follow it.

YOURS FOR JUST $29.50*
One jacket   just $35.95
Two jackets   just $71.90
Three jackets just $29.50
each when you buy three or more

LeatherGuy Inc.

423 Gerome Avenue Plato, Pennsylvania 18452

Leather Guy Jacket $29.50 each (when you buy three)

Yes! Send _____ jacket(s). I enclose $ _____

purchase price, plus $3.25 postage for each jacket.

Sizes (please circle) S   M   L   XL   XXL

☐ Check enclosed   ☐ Visa   ☐ MasterCard   ☐ Discover

Card # _____   Exp.: ___/___

Mr./Mrs./Ms. _____

Address_____

City/State_____Zip_____

Order Fast: Call 1-800-800-Guys or Order on line at www.xxxxxx.com

1. To get one jacket for $29.50, you must buy at least
   a one.   **b** three.   **c** two.

2. Three jackets would cost a total of:
   a $88.50   **b** $71.90   **c** $320.00

3. What is the postage fee for mailing two jackets?
   a $3.25   **b** $6.50   **c** $6.25

Write the answers to questions 4–6 on the lines below.

4. What's the difference between a savings account and a checking account?

   _____

   _____

   _____

5. Suppose that Murray has just graduated from high school. He has a new job, and is sharing an apartment with two friends. Murray wants a charge card of some kind, but can't decide whether it should be a **credit card** or a **debit card**. What would you advise Murray to do? Explain why.

   _____

   _____

   _____

   _____

   _____

   _____

6. What's the most important thing you've learned in Section 2? Explain why it's important to you.

   _____

   _____

   _____

   _____

Reading to Get and Give Information

You can probably guess what a *close reader* is: someone who reads important information carefully, sentence by sentence, word by word, and sometimes more than once. *Close reading* is always a good idea, but it's especially important in the situations you'll work with in this section. For example, you read closely to:

- Learn **exactly** how to use medicine.

- Find the **exact** name or word you need in a phone book or dictionary.

- See how to fill out forms **exactly** as directed.

In this section, you'll build your close-reading skills. You'll also practice writing careful answers to questions.

Contents

1. Reading About How to Use Medicine

Medicines come with directions about how to use them. If you don't use the medicine according to the directions, here's what might happen:

- The medicine won't do what it was made to do.
- The medicine may harm you.

There are lots of medicines that you can buy *over the counter*. That means you can buy them *without* a doctor's **prescription**, or **written form from a doctor**. An over-the-counter medicine has directions on the bottle or box. Read the directions to find out:

- **What** the medicine is supposed to do.
- **Who** can use the medicine.
- **When** and **how** to use the medicine.

who can use the medicine

what the medicine is for

how to use the medicine

how long and when to use the medicine

Directions: For adults, and children 4 years of age and older.
Use: For minor cuts, scrapes, scratches, itches, and insect bites.
How to use: Use clean gauze or cotton to apply Skin-Ease to affected area.
Caution: 1. Do not apply more than five times in 24 hours.
2. If irritation persists after 3 days, see your doctor.
3. For external use only.

when you might need a doctor for help

Words and Meanings

affected area—the part that needs care
apply—put on
caution—warning
external—outside; not to be swallowed or eaten
irritation—a soreness or itch
minor—not very serious
persists—goes on; continues

1. The picture at right shows a bottle of MERTHIOLATE. Merthiolate is a

   a kind of soda.
   b medicine for your skin.
   c pill to take by mouth.

2. You could use Merthiolate if you

   a break your arm.
   b scrape your knee.
   c have a headache.

3. How often should you use Merthiolate?

   a for several weeks
   b every hour
   c 1 to 3 times a day

4. **If pain or irritation continues** means

   a if your cut stops hurting.
   b if you get another cut.
   c if your cut keeps hurting.

5. Which words tell you not to **drink** Merthiolate?

   a Alcohol—50% by volume.
   b For external use only.
   c 1 fl. oz.

6. **Keep out of reach of children** means

   a Put Merthiolate where kids can't get to it.
   b Use Merthiolate only with children over 5 years old.
   c Use Merthiolate only on children's scrapes and cuts.

Tincture Merthiolate

1:1000
Sodium Ethyl Mercuri Thiosalicylate
(Thimerosal, Lily)
Alcohol–50% by volume

FOR EXTERNAL USE ONLY

A FIRST-AID ANTISEPTIC
1 FL. OZ.

Directions: Apply to affected area one to three times daily. Use: For cuts and scrapes.
Caution: I. For external use only.
2. If pain or irritation continues beyond 1 week, see your doctor.
3. Keep out of reach of children.

Write your answers on the lines below.

7. Suppose a friend says, "You should really try *Fantasmo*! You can get it over the counter at the drugstore." Finish the questions you would ask your friend.

What _____

_____?

Why _____

_____?

Who _____

_____?

How _____

_____?

2. Reading Directions for Prescription Medicine

Sometimes you need a medicine that you can't get over the counter. You need a doctor's prescription. A **prescription** is a written direction by a doctor. It tells what medicine to take and how often to take it. The prescription takes two forms:

- One is the doctor's form that you take to the drugstore and give to the pharmacist. Don't even try to figure it out! It's written in a form that only the doctor and the pharmacist can understand.

- The other is the label on the medicine that the drugstore gives you. This is the label that you must **read carefully!** Here's an example of a pharmacist's label on a prescription for a customer:

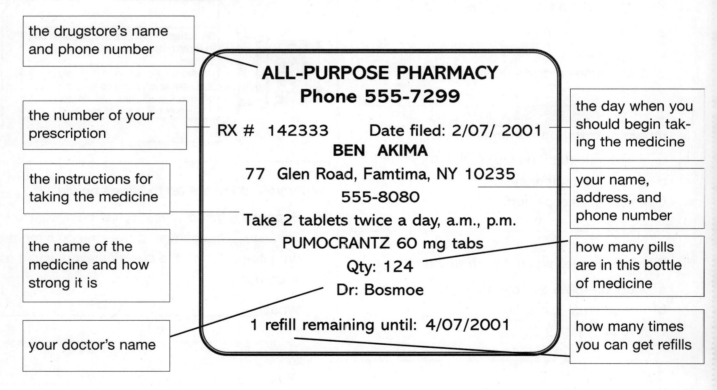

the drugstore's name and phone number

the number of your prescription

the instructions for taking the medicine

the name of the medicine and how strong it is

your doctor's name

ALL-PURPOSE PHARMACY
Phone 555-7299

RX # 142333   Date filed: 2/07/ 2001
BEN AKIMA
77 Glen Road, Famtima, NY 10235
555-8080
Take 2 tablets twice a day, a.m., p.m.
PUMOCRANTZ 60 mg tabs
Qty: 124
Dr: Bosmoe

1 refill remaining until: 4/07/2001

the day when you should begin taking the medicine

your name, address, and phone number

how many pills are in this bottle of medicine

how many times you can get refills

For a lot of people, a confusing part of the label on medicine is the part that starts **Take**. Take refers to *how many*. On the label above, it says *Take 2*. How often do you take 2 tablets? **Twice a day** means you take two tablets at different times of the day. In this case, you would take two in the morning (a.m.), and two at night (p.m.).

Read the label on the medicine below to find the answers. Write your answers on the lines.

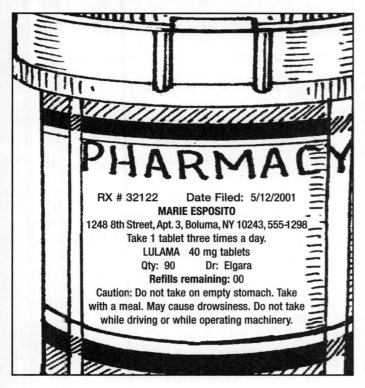

RX # 32122   Date Filed: 5/12/2001
MARIE ESPOSITO
1248 8th Street, Apt. 3, Boluma, NY 10243, 555-1298
Take 1 tablet three times a day.
LULAMA   40 mg tablets
Qty: 90   Dr: Elgara
Refills remaining: 00
Caution: Do not take on empty stomach. Take with a meal. May cause drowsiness. Do not take while driving or while operating machinery.

1. What is the name of the medicine Marie will be taking?

   _____

   _____

2. How many tablets will she take **each day**?

   _____

   _____

3. How many Lulama tablets are in the bottle?

   _____

   _____

4. Who is Marie's doctor?

   _____

5. How many refills are left? _____

   _____

6. Should Marie take her medicine just before she goes to bed at midnight, or right after she eats supper? Explain why.

   _____

   _____

   _____

7. **Drowsiness** means **feeling sleepy**. Why *shouldn't* Marie take a Lulama pill just before she drives to work?

   _____

   _____

   _____

8. If Marie needs more Lulama, to whom will she have to speak?_____

   _____

   Explain why.

   _____

   _____

   _____

3. Following Steps in a Process

When you follow directions to make or do something, you are following a process. A process is a series of steps that leads to a result. For example, there is a process you go through to get a driver's license, or to take a class at school. One of the most common processes of all is cooking or preparing a meal. The process is written down as a recipe. The recipe steps must be followed exactly.

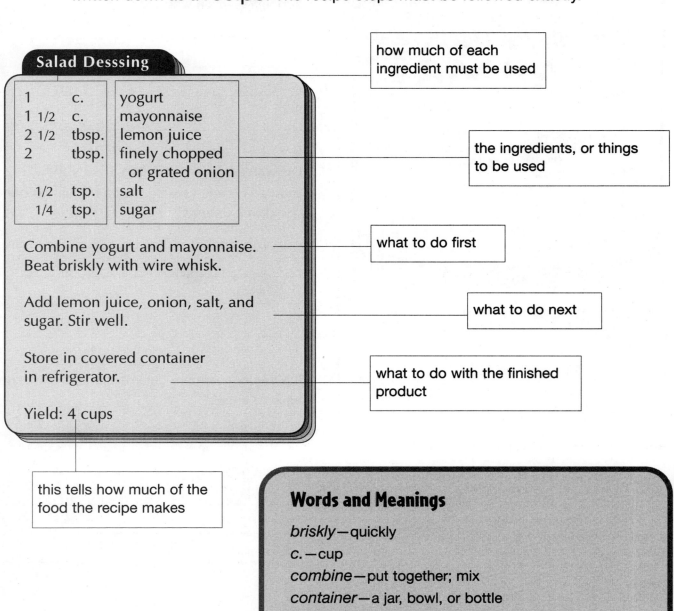

Salad Desssing

1	c.	yogurt
1 1/2	c.	mayonnaise
2 1/2	tbsp.	lemon juice
2	tbsp.	finely chopped or grated onion
1/2	tsp.	salt
1/4	tsp.	sugar

Combine yogurt and mayonnaise. Beat briskly with wire whisk.

Add lemon juice, onion, salt, and sugar. Stir well.

Store in covered container in refrigerator.

Yield: 4 cups

how much of each ingredient must be used

the ingredients, or things to be used

what to do first

what to do next

what to do with the finished product

this tells how much of the food the recipe makes

Words and Meanings

briskly—quickly
c.—cup
combine—put together; mix
container—a jar, bowl, or bottle
ingredients—foods used in a recipe
recipe—directions for making something to eat
tbsp.—tablespoon
tsp.—teaspoon
yield—the amount of food made

Refer to the recipe at the right to find the answers.

1. How many different ingredients does this recipe call for?

   a 6   **b** 5   **c** 8

2. In step 1, you

   a mix all the ingredients together.
   b put the ingredients in order.
   c mix the sugar and gelatin.

3. In step 2, you

   a dissolve boiling water.
   b pour boiling water into the sugar and gelatin.
   c put boiling water into a cup.

Cheesecake

1	envelope unflavored gelatin
1/2 c.	sugar
1 c.	boiling water
2	8-oz. packages cream cheese, softened
1 tsp.	vanilla extract
1	9-inch graham cracker crust

DIRECTIONS:

In a large bowl, mix gelatin with sugar. — **step 1**

Add boiling water and stir until completely dissolved. — **step 2**

With an electric mixer, beat in cream cheese and vanilla until smooth. — **step 3**

Pour into the crust and chill until firm. — **step 4**

Optional: Garnish with fresh or canned fruit. — **step 5**

Makes 8 servings.

---

4. In step 3, you add cream cheese and vanilla to the mixture and

   a put it into the refrigerator.
   b mix things together until they are smooth.
   c add the gelatin.

5. The mixture becomes firm

   a when it gets cold.
   b as you pour it into the crust.
   c as you beat it.

6. In step 5, what's the best meaning for *optional?*

   a important
   b necessary
   c not necessary

7. In step 5, what does *garnish* mean?

   a put on top
   b remove
   c serve on separate plates

8. The cheesecake is just enough for

   a three people.
   b twelve people.
   c eight people.

4. Using a Dictionary

As you probably know, a dictionary gives the **meanings** and correct **spelling** of words. In addition, the dictionary:

- Tells how to **pronounce**, or say, the word.

- Gives the many **different meanings** a word may have.

- Tells whether the word is a noun, a verb, an adjective, or an adverb.

The words in a dictionary are listed in alphabetical order. For example, the word *zest* comes after *zap* and before *zip*.

Here's an example of the top part of a dictionary page:

Guide word, right: This tells the *last* word on this dictionary page.

Guide word, left: This tells the *first* word on this dictionary page.

This tells the correct pronunciation of the word. The dots separate the three syllables.

swim	symphony
swim (swim) *v.i.* to propel oneself in water by means of hands, feet, or fins, etc.; to float on surface; to move with gliding motion, resembling swimming; *v.t.* to cross or pass over by swimming; to cause to swim; *n.* act of swimming; spell of swimming. *pr.p.* **-ming.** *pa.p.* **swum.** *pa.t.* **swam. -mer** *n.* **-mingly** *adv.* easily, successfully	**syc•o•phant** (sik´•a•fant) *n.* flatterer, or one who fawns on rich or famous; parasite; *adj.* servile;. **sychophancy** *n.* **-ic, -ical, -ically** *adv.* **-ish** *adj.*
swin•dle (swin´•dl) *v.t.* and *v.i.* to cheat or defraud; to obtain by fraud; *n.* act of defrauding	**syl•la•ble** (sil´•a•bl) *n.* sound uttered at single effort of voice, and constituting word, or part of word; *v.t.* to utter in syllables; to articulate. **syllabic, syllabical** *adj.* pert. to, or consisting of, a syllable. **syllabically** *adv.* **syllabicate, syllabize,** *v.t.* to divide into syllables

This means the word is usually used as a noun.

Here are the different meanings of the word.

This gives the correct spelling of the word.

Words and Meanings

adj. — adjective

adv. — adverb

n. — noun

pronunciation — saying the word correctly

A. On the lines, write the following words in alphabetical order. Some words start with the same letter. You will have to look at the second or third letters in these words.

harvest	mother	last
distance	pitch	pity
escape	disturb	least
patch	worry	morning

1. _____   7. _____

2. _____   8. _____

3. _____   9. _____

4. _____   10. _____

5. _____   11. _____

6. _____   12. _____

B. Look below at the guide words from a dictionary page. Then look at **Words to List**. Put the words in the right order under the guide words. Remember, the guide word on the *left* is the *first* word on the page. The guide word on the right is the *last* word on the page.

pound	practical
pound _____	_____
_____	_____
_____	_____
_____	_____
_____	*practical*

Words to List

prohibit	progress	profuse
program	progeny	profusion

C. Read each sentence. Choose the best meaning for the underlined word. Circle your choice.

1. A new <u>wave</u> of students will enter this year.
   a moving hand
   b moving water
   c group

2. Their names are alphabetized on the <u>roll</u> at the office.
   a official list
   b push over
   c kind of bread

3. The <u>principle</u> course I am taking is Law Enforcement.
   a head of a school
   b rule
   c most important

4. There is a <u>current</u> need for more protection in the city.
   a present time
   b flowing water
   c electric power

■ **Now use a dictionary to find the different meanings of each underlined word. Correct any mistakes you may have made.**

5. Using a Telephone Book

Most telephone books have three main sections.

■ **First** comes a list of Emergency Numbers. The list usually appears like this:

Emergency Numbers
POLICE 911
FIRE.................................911-0248
AMBULANCE.....................555-7000

■ Next there are many, many pages of **individual listings**. These are the telephone numbers and brief addresses for people and companies. The listings are in alphabetical order by name.

Names of people and companies are listed in alphabetical order. In some cities, people and companies are listed in separate sections.

A person's last name is shown first

Colbert Jane	61–67 Austin St.	555-9484
Coldwell Inc.	85–88 Lefferts Blvd.	555-6990
Coleman Eve	50 86th Ave.	555-1934
Coleman R	7643 Queens Blvd.	555-5720

Usually, street addresses are given.

■ In a separate section or book are the Yellow Pages. These are listings for companies, stores, and services. Here, the listings are in alphabetical order according to the *category*, or kind of thing being offered.

Notice that the listings within each category are in alphabetical order, too.

LAUNDRIES
Adams Laundry and Dry Cleaning	63 State 555-6050
Petunia's Clean-Up	412 West Grand 555-3040
Valley Valets	9–14 Bizne Blvd. 555-7070

LAWN CARE
| Mo's Mow-and-Grow | Route 75. ....555-3255 |
| Rolling Mowers | Route 75A .... 555-2829 |

LIBRARIES
| Edgemont Community Library | 10 Partition Street .... 555-4545 |
| Henry Street Children's Library | 112 Maxwell Ave ..... 555-7877 |

Refer to the phone book listings on the right to find the answers to the questions below. Circle your answers.

1. You see smoke coming out of your neighbor's house. Which number will you call?

   a 555-7777   **b** 911   **c** 555-2222

2. Which number will you call to report that your house was broken into?

   a 911   **b** 555-1722   **c** 411

3. You want to call a friend in Enid. The area code is 405, and the number is 555-3105. Your area code is 415. You should dial

   a 1+405+555-3105.
   b 1+7+715+555-3105.
   c 1+405+1234.

4. By mistake, Hickel's Market delivered a package to you labeled *Hill*. You don't know where this particular Hill family lives. What number will you call?

   a 411   **b** 555-3206   **c** 555-2904

5. You want Hillside Cabs to send you a cab. What number will you call?

   a 555-3206   **b** 555-1111   **c** 555-8960

6. You want to call Mrs. H. Hill on Platt Place. What number will you dial?

   a 555-2905   **b** 555-3940   **c** 555-1105

7. You can't find the number you want in the telephone book. For help, call

   a 411.   **b** 555-7777.   **c** 911.

EMERGENCY NUMBERS

Police, Ambulance, Fire 911

Medical Emergencies
Emergency Rescue Squad 555-1722

Hospitals
Governors Hospital 555-7777
Mt. Mary's Hospital 555-1101

Power and Utilities
All-County Electric 555-9090
Gas Leaks 555-2222

Information 411

LOCAL CALLS:
• For calls within your area code, just dial 7 digits. Example: 555+1234.

LONG DISTANCE CALLS:
• For calls outside your area code, dial 1 + **area code** + 7 digits. Example: 1 + **666** + 555-1234

Hi-Tech Roofers	11 Main Ave. 555-8885
Hickel Jos	22 S. 18th St. 555-6747
Hickel's Market	195 Rorer Rd. 555-3206
Higgins Arthur	25 Myrtle Ave. 555-5291
Hill Gloria	292 N. Wood St. 555-2120
Hill H.D.	622 Pine Blvd. 555-3026
Hill Harry	32 S. 9th St. 555-2904
Hill Harry	134 Platt Pl. 555-3940
Hill Hattie	6409 Bath Pl. 555-1105
Hillo Saml.	41 Thayer Ave. 555-1015
Hillside Cabs	63 20th St. 555-1111
Hill Star Video	28 Main Ave. 555-8960

6. Using a Table of Contents and an Index

A **table of contents** is a list of the chapters or sections in a book, in the order in which they appear. The table of contents also tells the page on which a chapter begins.

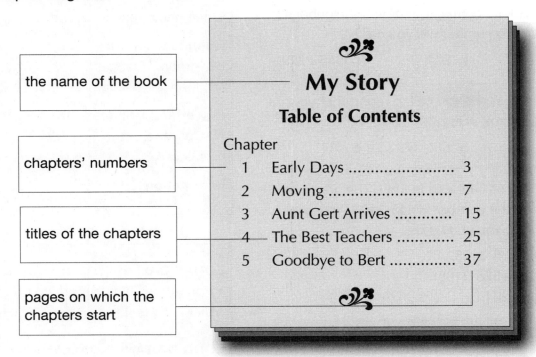

the name of the book

chapters' numbers

titles of the chapters

pages on which the chapters start

My Story

Table of Contents

Chapter

Some books also have an **index**. An index is in the back of the book. It lists the different topics in the book in *alphabetical order*. Then it gives the different page numbers where you can find information on the topic.

Words and Meanings

chapter—a section or part of a book

contents—what's in the book

index—an alphabetical list of the book's contents

table of contents—a list of chapter titles in the order in which they appear

Use what you've learned.

Refer to the index on this page to answer questions 1–5. Circle the answers you choose.

1. The index lists the headings and the topics
   a according to page number.
   b alphabetically.
   c according to importance.

2. On which page in the book can you find information about down payments?
   a 396   b 12   c 63

3. You want information about chemicals used in dry cleaning. You will look on page:
   a 203   b 280   c 183

4. Information about **driver's licenses** comes
   a before information about **dividends**.
   b after information about **dividends**.
   c in the listing for **dividends**.

5. Under which section will you find *radios* listed?
   a Decorating
   b Electricity
   c Entertainment appliances

6. **List the chapters and page numbers in the right order in the Table of Contents.**

Table of Contents

Chapter

1_____ . . . . . ____

2_____ . . . . . ____

3_____ . . . . . ____

4_____ . . . . . ____

5_____ . . . . . ____

Vocabulary

Look in the box. Find the meaning for each word and write it on the correct line.

1. prescription _____

2. over-the-counter _____

3. twice _____

4. ingredients _____

5. tbsp. _____

6. pronunciation _____

7. table of contents _____

8. index _____

9. caution _____

10. minor _____

11. apply _____

12. persists _____

tablespoon

not very serious

alphabetical list of topics

without a prescription

two times

warning

how a word is said

the parts of a book, in order

put on

goes on

written form from a doctor

foods used in a recipe

Comprehension

Write your answers to the questions.

1. What's the *safest* way to learn how to use medicine? Explain **why** this is the safest way.

_____

_____

_____

_____

_____

2. For *you*, what are the most important parts of a dictionary entry? Explain how you use these parts.

_____

_____

_____

_____

_____

3. Alphabetical order isn't used in a recipe. What kind of order **is** used in a recipe?

_____

_____

_____

_____

_____

4. Choose one of the words below. Write it on this line: _____

light   close   track   fat   ward

Now use a dictionary to find **at least two** meanings for the word you chose. It's great if you can find *more* than two. Write the different meanings on the lines below.

_____

_____

_____

_____

_____

7. Reading Graphs

Graphs show information **visually**, or in a way you can **see**. They give information with lines, bars, circles, or special drawings and pictures. Here are some examples of different kinds of graphs:

A Line Graph

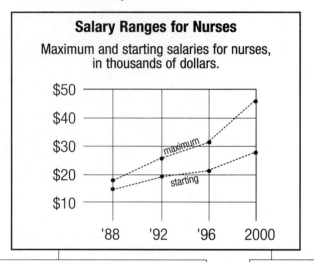

This **line graph** uses lines to compare salaries in different years.

A Bar Graph

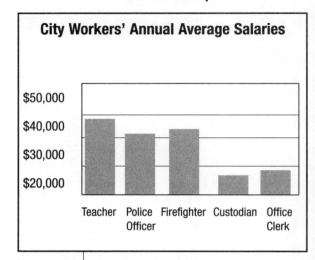

To read **line graphs** and **bar graphs**, read *across* (left to right) and *up* (bottom to top).

A Circle Graph

This **circle graph** shows amounts in percents (%). The percents must add up to 100%.

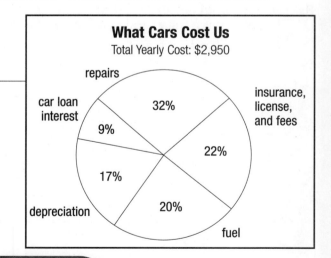

Words and Meanings

annual—yearly

average—normal; middle point

depreciation—decrease in value

miscellaneous (misc.)—odds and ends; an assortment of things

percent (%)—a part of a total amount

Study the bar graph to find the answers.

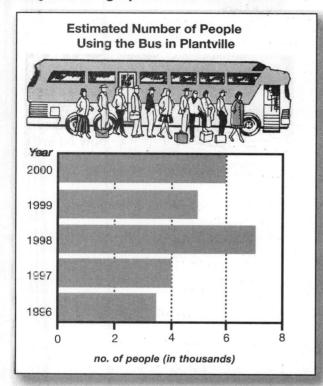

Estimated Number of People Using the Bus in Plantville

no. of people (in thousands)

Study the circle graph to find the answers.

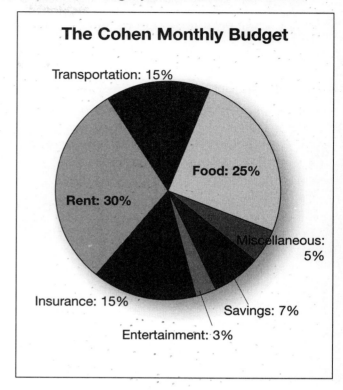

The Cohen Monthly Budget

1. The numbers along the *bottom* of the chart stand for the

   a number of bus riders.
   b years being compared.
   c number of buses.

2. At the bottom of the chart, **8** stands for:

   a eight thousand.
   b eight hundred.
   c eight years.

3. How many people used the bus in 1997?

   a 4,000   b 3,500   c 34,000

4. What is **not** true about bus travel in Plantville in 2000?

   a About six thousand people rode the bus.
   b More people rode the bus than in 1999.
   c More passengers used the bus than ever before.

5. This circle graph tells you

   a the total amount of money (dollars) the Cohens spend each month.
   b what percent of their money the Cohens spend on certain things.
   c how much money the Cohens must earn each month.

6. What *two* items make up 55% of the budget?

   a transportation and food
   b food and insurance
   c food and rent

7. For what item is the *least* amount of money budgeted?

   a savings
   b insurance
   c entertainment

8. If the Cohens earn $4,000 each month, how much money do they plan to spend on miscellaneous expenses?

   a $200   b $400   c $1,000

8. Reading Test Directions

All written tests have **directions** you're supposed to follow. The directions tell you what you must do. When taking a test, follow the directions carefully. You usually have to do several things.

Here's an example from a school test:

Directions: Read the story and the questions that follow it. Choose the best answer to each question. In the answer box, mark the space for your answer choice.

The test taker must:

1. READ something
2. CHOOSE something
3. FIND something (the answer box)
4. WRITE a check mark or "x" in the box

Here's an example from a driver's license written test:

Directions: Print and sign your full name, as it appears on your application for a license. Read and answer all the questions on the examination. Place the letter of your answer in the answer box at the lower right of each question.

The test taker must:

1. PRINT and SIGN something
2. READ and ANSWER something
3. PLACE something
4. FIND where to place something

Words and Meanings

answer box—the place on a test paper where you put a mark for your answer

best answer—the answer that is most accurate and true of all the choices

examination—test

mark—a mark in a box to show your answer (usually a "✓" or an "x")

print—write in separate letters. Don't join the letters.

Follow the directions below carefully! They are different from the directions you've followed on other pages.

1. **Before you write anything**, just **read** questions 2 and 3 below. *Then* answer question 4.

2. Print your last name and the initial of your first name inside the boxes.

   LAST NAME   FIRST NAME INITIAL

3. Circle the number of this page.

72	73	74	75	76	77	78	79	80	81	82	83

4. Circle the answer that tells what you did.

   a I followed the directions in 1, and didn't write anything yet for 2 and 3.

   b I didn't follow the directions in 1, because I've already answered 2 and 3.

5. Now answer questions 2 and 3. Then go on to question 6, below.

6. Look at the dark number at the left of each row. Circle the number in that row that is the same.

563	653	356	563	593
1290	1190	2190	1129	1290

7. In each row, circle the words that are the same.

   enter entrance either enter eaten

   lend lane lend lent line let

   can cane cain can canned can't

The directions below are for marking answers on a test. Follow the directions.

8. In each row, fill in the answer space with the same number or letters that you see to the left of the row.

Follow the directions.

9. The correct answer is given at the left of each row. Look at the way the answer spaces have been marked. Put a check (✓) inside the box at the left if the answer is correctly marked.

9. Filling Out a Job Application

Before you can get a job, you'll probably have to fill out a **job application.** A big part of getting a job depends on how well you fill out the application. Look at what facts are required. Enter the answers as fully and neatly as you can.

Application forms are all different, but here's a typical one:

Don't write in script.

Give the month, day, and year.

Give your Social Security number.

Follow the right order in printing your name.

Say the kind of job you want.

This means part-time hours—if you want a part-time job.

APPLICATION FOR EMPLOYMENT

(please print or type)

Date _____

1. Name _____ Soc. Sec. # _____
   Last   First   Middle

2. Present Address _____
   Street   City/Town   State   Zip

3. a) Position Desired or Applying For _____
   b) Full-time ☐   Part-time ☐   From_____ To _____

4. a) Minimum Salary Required _____   b) Date Available for Work _____

5. Name of any Friend or Relative in the Company _____

Words and Meanings

apply for—ask for; fill out forms for

available—ready to begin

bus.—business

desired—wanted

employment—job

minimum salary required—smallest amount of pay you'll take

previous, previously—before this time

P/T—part-time

Soc. Sec. #—Social Security number

1. In the application form on page 84, what should you **not** do?

   a print the information

   b write the information in longhand

   c use a pen

2. In part 6 on the form at the right, what is question **a** asking?

   a Are you looking for a job?

   b Have you worked before?

   c Have you ever been fired from a job?

3. In part 6 of the form, what is question **b** asking?

   a Do you like working?

   b Have you worked before?

   c Have you ever asked for a job before?

4. In part 6, what are questions **c** and **d** about?

   a the work you did before

   b your heath

   c your education

5. In part 7 of the form, what will you write about the schools you went to?

   a the names, the dates, and if you finished

   b the names, the places, the dates, and if you finished

   c just the places, the dates, and if you finished

JOB APPLICATION FORM

Previous Work and Health History

6.	Have you ever previously:	Yes	No
	a) been employed?		
	b) applied for employment?		
	c) had or do you now have any physical defects, limitations, or chronic ailments?		
	d) had or do you now have any serious ailment?		

Education

7.	School Name City/State	Dates Attended		Graduated	
		From	To	Yes	No
	a) High School City/State				
	b) College/University City/State				
	c) Bus./Tech. School City/State				

8. Technical or business skills (including training and special courses with dates)

   _____

Suppose you are applying for a job. On the application form, you are asked to write your answers to the following questions. Write the answers.

6. Describe the kind of job you'd like to have.

   _____

   _____

   _____

   _____

   _____

7. What are your special skills and strengths?

   _____

   _____

   _____

   _____

10. Reading and Writing Memos

A **memo** is a short message that gives only the most *important information in a small space.* Memos are used mainly in workplaces. They're also used at home and school.

Here's a memo written in an office:

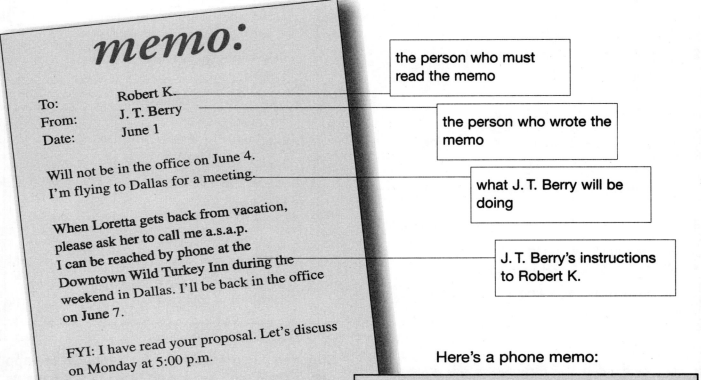

memo:

To: Robert K.
From: J. T. Berry
Date: June 1

Will not be in the office on June 4.
I'm flying to Dallas for a meeting.

When Loretta gets back from vacation, please ask her to call me a.s.a.p. I can be reached by phone at the Downtown Wild Turkey Inn during the weekend in Dallas. I'll be back in the office on June 7.

FYI: I have read your proposal. Let's discuss on Monday at 5:00 p.m.

the person who must read the memo

the person who wrote the memo

what J. T. Berry will be doing

J. T. Berry's instructions to Robert K.

special note from J. T. Berry to Robert K.

Here's a phone memo:

While You Were Out

Date *July 8*   Time *2:30 p.m.*
To: *Jen*
Caller: *Madison Sommers*
Message: *Has an apartment you might like.*
Call 555-1800 before 6 pm.
Jeanette ☺

Words and Meanings

a.s.a.p. —as soon as possible

FYI—**F**or **Y**our **I**nformation

memo—short for memorandum. A memorandum is a short message.

To answer questions 1–4, study the memo from J. T. Berry on page 86.

1. Who gets the memo?

   a J. T. Berry
   b Loretta
   c Robert K.

2. When will J. T. Berry be back in the office?

   a June 7
   b June 1
   c June 4

3. According to the memo, what should Robert K. do?

   a call the Downtown Wild Turkey Inn
   b be back in the office by June 7th
   c ask Loretta to call J. T. Berry as soon as possible

4. The FYI note

   a tells where the Downtown Wild Turkey Inn is located.
   b sets up a time for a meeting.
   c tells when J. T. Berry will return from his trip.

To answer questions 5–7, study the memo on this page.

ANTELOPE INC.

J. T. Berry
Executive V. P.

To: Robert K.
Date: Oct. 6
Subject: AAA Order

AAA Shoe Company wants Model 2615 in Blue. They want 50 pairs of this model delivered by next Tuesday. Give them a call. Say you can ship 20 pairs by tomorrow and 30 pairs in two weeks. If they agree, ship the order by Express Mail.

Notify Subodh in Manufacturing. Make him promise 30 pairs of #2615 by the 14th.

FYI
AAA moved to a new location.
When you call—ask for their exact address.

---

5. Who wrote the memo?

   a Robert K.
   b J. T. Berry.
   c AAA Shoe Company.

6. Who must read the memo?

   a Robert K.
   b AAA Shoe Company
   c Mr. Subodh in manufacturing

7. What is the main message in the memo?

   a why AAA moved to a new location
   b the color of the shoes that Antelope Inc. makes
   c how to discuss shoe deliveries with AAA

8. Use the form below to write a memo on one of these subjects:

   school work   shopping
   chores   around the house

   From:
   To:
   Date:
   Subject:
   Message: _____

   _____

   _____

   _____

   _____

   _____

   _____

   _____

   _____

11. Applying for a Loan

Banks and lending institutions lend money to people who **qualify**, or can prove that they are able to pay back the money borrowed. In order to apply for a loan, you will have to fill out a **loan application form**, like the one below.

Own Home ☐ Mortgage Payment (monthly) $_____	If you own your house, put a check mark here.
Value_____	Give the correct amount.
Rent Home ☐ Monthly Payment $_____	If you rent your house, give the name of your landlord.
Landlord or mortgage holder_____	If you borrowed money to buy your house, give the name of the bank that loaned you the money.
Employer_____	Write the name and address of the person or company you work for.
Address_____	
Your Position_____	Tell what kind of job you do.
No. of years_____ Monthly Salary_____	Tell how much you earn each month at your job.
Credit References (name, address) _____	Write the names and addresses of your bank and of your credit card companies.

Things to remember:

- Banks and lending institutions will contact almost everyone from whom you've borrowed money before. Did you pay on time? Or, did you borrow way over your head, so that you couldn't pay your debts? A bank will lend you money only if you have a good record.

- Banks don't lend money for free. A loan comes with *interest*. Interest is the extra fee you give the bank each month for the privilege of borrowing money.

Words and Meanings

mortgage—money borrowed from a bank to pay for a house

previous—past; former; earlier

value—how much something is worth

Look at the Application for a Car Loan at right to answer questions 1–4. Circle the answers you choose.

1. If you pay a mortgage to a bank, on which line will you write the bank's name?

   a Monthly Payment

   b Credit References

   c Landlord or Mortgage Holder

2 Which one could you use as a credit reference?

   a Your neighborhood theater

   b A grocery store where you have a charge account

   c Your nearest relative

3. If you are asked for your signature, you will

   a type your full name.

   b print the letters of your full name.

   c write your name in longhand.

4. In his last job, Jim worked for Parson's TV Company. This means that Parson's is Jim's

   a previous employer.

   b present employer.

   c credit reference.

5. On the form at the right, fill in the following details:

   Teresa Milan wants to take out a loan to buy Ms. Elvira Nolan's 1992 Honda. Teresa rents an apartment from J. B. Goode at 94 State Street, in your city. She pays $550 a month for rent. She has been working for a year for Jones Auto Sales as a bookkeeper. She earns $500 a week. Teresa used to work for Kenny's Clothing as a salesperson, and she still has a charge account there. Teresa has a checking account at the Nickle Bank and Trust Company on Main Street.

Application for a Car Loan

Name _____

Address _____

City, State, & Zip _____

Home Phone Number _____

Own Home ☐   Mortgage Payment (monthly) $ _____

Value _____

Rent Home ☐   Monthly Payment $ _____

Landlord or Mortgage Holder _____

Address _____

Employer _____

Address _____

Your Position_____

No. of Years_____ Salary _____

Previous Address (if less than 3 years) _____

_____

Previous Employer (if less than 3 years) _____

_____

Credit References (name, address) _____

_____

_____

Car Make _____Year_____

Title Held By _____

Your Bank Name _____

Your Branch Address_____

Type of Account: ☐ Savings   ☐ Checking   ☐ Loan

Social Security Number _____

Driver's License No._____State_____

Date of Birth _____

Name and Address of Relative Not Living With You:

_____

I represent that each of the statements contained in this application is true and correct. I authorize anyone referred to herein to furnish the bank such information as may be required in connection with the application, and agree that the application remains the property of the bank, whether or not this loan is granted.

Signature_____

Vocabulary

Look in the box. Find the meaning for each word and write it on the correct lines.

1. graph _____

2. minimum _____

3. mortgage _____

4. percent _____

5. combine _____

6. chapter _____

7. examination _____

8. available _____

9. annual _____

10. recipe _____

11. print _____

12. value _____

yearly

directions for making a meal

write in separate letters

test

a section or part of a book

smallest

a way of giving information visually

worth

ready

put together

money borrowed to pay for a house

a part of a total

Comprehension

Follow the directions to complete the two activities.

Fill in the form below with your information.

Job Application Form

Today's Date _____

Your Name _____
               last   first

Your Address _____
               street   apt. #, if any

_____
     city or town   state   zip

Daytime Phone _____

Date of Birth _____
          month   day   year

Check the job you are applying for. Check one only.

☐ receptionist

☐ health club manager

☐ car valet service

☐ other (Please be specific.) _____

_____

_____

Describe the work you do in your present job.

_____

_____

_____

_____

_____

_____

_____

How long have you been working at your
present job? _____

The circle graph below shows what percentage of the people in Waystock attend the town's special events. For example, 12% of the residents either watch or take part in the Road Race. Refer to the graph to answer the questions.

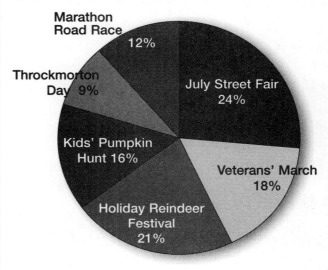

Marathon Road Race 12%
Throckmorton Day 9%
July Street Fair 24%
Kids' Pumpkin Hunt 16%
Veterans' March 18%
Holiday Reindeer Festival 21%

a Which event is the most popular?

_____

b Which event is the least popular?

_____

c What percent of the community turns up for the Pumpkin Hunt?

_____

d About 25% of the people in Waystock celebrate which event?

_____

e Which event is more popular?

1. The Road Race   2. The Pumpkin Hunt

ANSWER KEY

Section 1

page 9

1. c   2. c   3. c   4. a   5. c   6. c
7. b   8. a: The car on the right.
8. b: The sign says "yield."

page 11

1. b   2. b   3. b   4. a   5. a   6. b
7. c   8. c

page 13

1. b   2. b   3. b   4. b
5. a: Only a bus can stop or wait here.
6. b: Car b is going the wrong way on a one-way street.

page 15

DRIVER'S LICENSE APPLICATION	FOR OFFICE USE ONLY

DRIVER'S LICENSE APPLICATION
Use blue or black ink only in the boxes.

FOR OFFICE USE ONLY
Batch file No.
T-code
LRC   LAM   LRN
LOP

A. LAST NAME: Yen   FIRST NAME: Mary   MIDDLE INITIAL: L

B. DATE OF BIRTH — Month 1 Day 2 Year 1989   SEX: M F̶   HEIGHT: Ft 5 Inches 4   EYE COLOR: Green   SOCIAL SECURITY NUMBER: 958-24-9687

C. MAILING ADDRESS *(Include Street Number and Name, Rural Delivery, Box and/or Apartment Number)*
5 Dulcimer Lane, Apartment A

CITY OR TOWN: Woodstock   STATE: NY   ZIP CODE: 12498   COUNTY: Ulster

D. Do you have or have you held a driver's license for this state?   ☑ No   ☐ Yes

If YES, write the license number.

E. Sign your name in full   *Mary Lee Yen*

page 17

1. a   2. b   3. a   4. a   5. b   6. c
7. c   8. c   9. a
10. Example answer: Keep walking east on Constitution Avenue. When you come to New Jersey Avenue, look to your right. You will see the House of Representatives.

page 19

1. a   2. a   3. c   4. b   5. a
6. c   7. b
8. F Street runs east to west between E Street and G Street.
9. 2nd Street runs from north to south between 1st Street and 3rd Street.
10. Different answers are possible. Example answer: I could walk to the Supreme Court Building. Then I could go to the U.S. Capitol and the House of Representatives. Then I'd hurry back to Union Station.

page 21

1. c   2. b   3. c   4.b   5. a   6. b
7. b
8. Answers will vary.

page 23

1. a   2. b   3. a   4. a
5. a: b: c:
6. directions; a place to camp

page 24

1. b   2. a   3. b   4. c   5. c   6. c
7. a   8. b   9. a   10. a   11. a   12. c

page 25

1. a: the white car
   b: The solid line means you should not pass.
2. a:
   b: Example answer: I would look at a road map.
3. right
4. Different answers are possible. Example answers:
   • The symbols can help you find your way easily.
   • You have to learn what the symbols mean.

page 27

1. b	2. a	3. a	4. b
5. b	6. b	7. c	8. a. 7:20A
			b. 9:35A
			c. 8:00P

page 29

1. b	2. c	3. b	4. a	5. b	6. b
7. a	8. 6:30 P; 647; 1 hour; some snacks				

page 31

1. c	2. b	3. c	4. b	5. a	6. c
7. a	8. b	9. c	10. b		

page 32

1. b	2. a	3. c	4. b	5. a	6. a
7. c	8. b				

page 33

1. c	2. a	3. b	4. c	5. a

6. Railroad crossing; No trucks allowed; Slippery when wet; You can get gasoline here; School children cross here.

Section 2

page 37

1. c	2. a	3. b	4. a	5. c	6. a
7. b	8. c	9. b			

page 39

1. $7.20; $10.35; $6.40; $8.98; $1.60

2. b	3. b	4. c	5. a

page 41

1. b	2. a	3. b	4. b	5. c	6. c

page 43

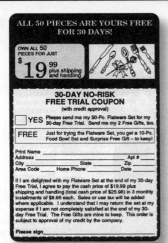

1.

a: You can keep these even if you decide to return the flatware set.

b: Check here if you accept this offer.

c: If you send the flatware back, you pay the postage.

d: If you keep the set, you may also have to pay sales tax.

e: This is what you'll pay altogether if you decide to keep the flatware.

2. Answers will vary. Example answers:
• Yes, I'd order it. I could check it out, and send it back if I didn't like it.
• No. There are too many catches. I think I would spend too much.
3. Answers will vary.
4. Answers will vary.
5. Answers will vary.

page 45

1.

#321A114	
Snuggle-In Jacket	#221C214
Sun-glow	Snow Cap
M	Brown
1	one size
$51.00	$12.98
$51.00	$12.98

2.

Z-L DEPARTMENT STORE

Please use this coupon
for mail orders   Date May 5, 2003

Item #	Description & Color	Size	Qty.	Unit Price	Total
738C12	Yellow	8	1	$16.50	$16.50
738D14	Brown	one size	2	$8.50	$17.00

☐ Charge my Visa/Mastercard

☒ Check or MO enclosed
   (DO NOT enclose CASH.)

☒ Gift Wrap

Subtotal	$33.50
If delivered in city, add 5% sales tax	

CHARGE TO:

Visa/Mastercard _____

Name _____

Address _____

City/State/Zip _____

SEND TO:

Name __Ellen Ramirez__

Address __P.O. Box #52__

City/State/Zip __Benson, Arizona 85602__

SATISFACTION GUARANTEED OR YOUR MONEY BACK.

page 47

1. a   2. c   3. c   4. c   5. c   6. b

page 49

1. b   2. c   3. b   4. a   5. a   6. c

7. b   8. a   9. Answers will vary.

page 50

1. b   2. a   3. a   4. c   5. c   6. yd

7. lb.   8. furn   9. qty   10. flr   11. oz.

12. MO   13. util   14. ea.   15. lr   16. bth

page 51

1. a   2. a   3. b   4. c   5. c

6. No. The job is from October to April.

7. Answers will vary. Example: Checking to make
   sure the heat is on. Cleaning. Taking care of pets
   and plants.

8. Your salary depends on your experience. You
   would decide on a fair salary with your employer.

9. b

page 53

1. a   2. b   3. c   4. a   5. a

6.

DEPOSIT SLIP

Nickle Bank and Trust Co.

Date April 10, 2002

Checking Account #   72664

Name Stella Uribe

		Dollars	Cents
Cash		$50	00
Checks	1	$25	60
	2	$100	00
	3		
	4		
Bank Use only	5		
	Total	$175	60

page 55

1. c   2. b   3. a   4. b   5. c   6. a

7. b   8. a

page 57

1. b   2. b   3. a   4. c   5. c

6. Example answer: With a debit card, you use
   money you already have. With a credit card, you
   borrow money.

7. Answers will vary.

8. Answers will vary. Example: From now on, don't
   use credit cards or debit cards. Use cash.

page 59

1. c   2. c   3. b   4. b   5. a

6. Answers will vary.

7. a. Answers will vary. Example: He could empty his
   savings account, or he could take $1,200 from his
   savings account and go to the limit on his credit and
   debit cards.

b. Answers will vary.

page 61

August Budget

Out:	Amount
Rent	$600.00
Utilities	$34.50
Food	$450.00
Clothes	$400.50
Transportation	$2,050.00
Medical	0
Credit Card Payments	$300.00
Total Out	$3,835.00
In:	0
Louise's Salary	$1,000.00
Lew's Salary	$1,000.00
Rent from Tenant	0
Total In	$2,000.00

2. $3,835　　　3. $2,000　　　4. a
5. Answers will vary. Example: Louise and Lew are spending much more than they earn. They are very much in debt. They should cut down on their vacation and clothing expenses.

page 62

1. c　　2. b　　3. b　　4. a　　5. c　　6. a
7. b　　8. c　　9. c　　10. a

page 63

1. b　　2. a　　3. b
4. A savings account pays you interest for money you keep in the bank. A checking account allows you to pay bills with money you have put into the account.
5. Answers will vary. Example: I'd advise Murray to get a debit card. That way, he is less likely to end up with big debts he can't pay.
6. Answers will vary.

Section 3

page 67

1. b　　2. b　　3. c　　4. c　　5. b　　6. a
7. Answers will vary. Examples: What is Fantasmo? Why should I try it? Who needs to use Fantasmo? How do you know it's safe?

page 69

1. Lulama　　2. 3　　3. 90
4. Dr. Elgara　　5. none
6. Right after she eats supper. The caution says, "Take with a meal."
7. She might get drowsy and have a car accident.
8. Her doctor. This is a prescription medicine.

page 71

1. a　　2. c　　3. b　　4. b　　5. a　　6. c
7. a　　8. c

page 73

A. 1. distance　　2. disturb　　3. escape
4. harvest　　5. last　　6. least
7. morning　　8. mother　　9. patch
10. pitch　　11. pity　　12. worry
B. profuse, profusion, progeny, program, progress, prohibit
C. 1. c　2. a　　3. c　　4. a

page 75

1. b　　2. a　　3. a　　4. b　　5. b　　6. b
7. a

page 77

1. b　　2. c　　3. c　　4. b　　5. c

6. Words and Power...8
   The Story Behind the Story...28
   From Reading to Writing...44
   Short Takes...56
   Writing It All Down...72

page 78

1. written form from a doctor
2. without a prescription

ANSWER KEY

page 78 cont.

3. two times
4. foods used in a recipe
5. tablespoon
6. how a word is said
7. the parts of a book, in order
8. alphabetical list of topics
9. warning
10. not very serious
11. put on
12. goes on

page 79

1. Answers will vary. Example: Read the instructions. Then you will know how much medicine to take and when to take it.
2. Answers will vary.
3. Sequential order. A recipe tells you what to do first, second, etc.
4. Answers will vary.

page 81

1. a   2. a   3. a   4. c   5. b
6. c   7. c   8. a

page 83

4. If you followed the directions in 1, you will choose a.
5. 2: Example: Perez Jorge V.
3: 83

6.

563	653	356	(563)	593
1290	1190	2190	(1129)	1290

7.
(enter) entrance either (enter) eaten
(lend) lane (lend) lent line let
(can) cane cain (can) canned can't

8.

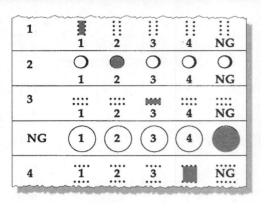

9. The third and fifth answers are correctly marked.

page 85

1. b   2. b   3. c   4. b   5. b
6. Answers will vary.   7. Answers will vary.

page 87

1. c   2. a   3. c   4. b   5. b   6. a
7. c   8. Answers will vary.

page 89

1. c   2. b   3. c   4. a
5. Check your completed form with a partner. Make corrections where they are needed.

page 90

1. a way of giving information visually
2. smallest
3. money borrowed to pay for a house
4. a part of a total
5. put together
6. a section or part of a book
7. test
8. ready
9. yearly
10. directions for making a meal
11. write in separate letters
12. worth

page 91

1. Answers will vary.
2. a. The July Street Fair
   b. Throckmorton Day
   c. 16%
   d. Veterans' March
   e. 2